Wave Good-bye to the Joneses

Wave Good-bye to the Joneses

THE CHRISTIAN USE OF WEALTH

James Breig

Fides/Claretian

Printed in the United States of America

ISBN 0-8190-0646-7

Cover design: Glenn Heinlein

Cover art: Don Pracht

LC 81-7828

First printing, July 1981

Fides/Claretian books are a series of books, published by the Claretian Fathers and Brothers, which examine the issue of Christian social justice in the United States. The books are written for grassroots Christians seeking social justice. They are based on the premise that it is not possible for everyone to do everything, but it is a Christian duty for everyone to do something.

For further information about Fides/Claretian, write to the address below.

Fides/Claretian

221 West Madison Street • Chicago, Illinois 60606

TO MY FAMILY,
FOR THEIR PATIENCE

Contents

Foreword

This is a book about the claims of social justice upon an affluent society. It not only calls for a modern-day application of the Judeo-Christian ethic; it provides practical guidelines to assist concerned citizens in meeting their obligations to their less-privileged fellow humans.

We live in a time when the "moral majority," the "Christian voice," and other like-minded groups are calling for commitment to such "moral" goals as a larger arms budget, the defeat of the Equal Rights Amendment, organized prayer sessions in the public schools, the rejection of the Panama Canal Treaty, and closer ties to Taiwan. Given these curious applications of "morality," it is refreshing to find James Breig calling upon Americans to heed the ancient biblical injunction to feed the hungry, heal the sick, comfort the afflicted, and assist the poor.

It is the thesis of this book that the obligation of those who are relatively affluent to those who are relatively poor is not a matter of charity; rather it is a matter of justice—the recognition of the right of every human being to share in the bounty of God's earth. The author knocks down the notion that because some are fabulously rich and are doing little to assist the less privileged that this greater disparity relieves the rest of us of our obligation to share our more modest affluence. As a U.S. senator, I frequently heard my colleagues argue that the new opulence of the OPEC states and industrial Japan has lifted the burden on our assisting the Third World. But the pages of this book make clear that so long as there are human beings in our society and abroad who have less than we do, the obligation to share remains.

This is not to say that we are under moral obligation to yield such comforts and advantages as a comfortable home, or a good education, or cultural pursuits in literature and the arts which enhance the human personality. It is to say that squandering our income on frivolous or harmful expenditures that do nothing to enrich personality while ignoring the most fundamental needs of others is not only a waste of resources, it diminishes us spiritually and deprives others of basic rights.

"We Americans who wonder where our tax money is going are the same ones who drink 90 million cans of beer a day. The same men and women who shake their heads over the price of gasoline smoke 1.6 billion cigarettes every 24 hours," writes Breig. We are also the same society that is preparing to spend one and a half trillion dollars on preparation for war in the next five years while hundreds of millions of our fellow humans cling to existence on the brink of starvation and misery.

In the pages which follow, the reader will be reminded that we must minister to "the wretched of the earth" whether or not it serves geopolitical ends.

There is presented here a blunt statement of the relative needs of the poor—largely located among the 100 nations that make up the Third World. There is also an analysis of the various forms of affluence with which most of us are endowed as Americans—material goods, natural resources, and the affluence of hope, security, opportunity, health, and freedom.

This is not a pessimistic book; it is based on an underlying faith in the Christian gospel and the potential capacity of the American people.

"We have been tested—as both Christians and Americans—and we have come through. We have made it through Vietnam, Watergate, and the Iranian hostages. . . . We have not come through without shame and fault. But . . . we have survived to hope for something better in the future," writes Breig.

"The ferment in our society, both our religious and political societies, is a sign of hope. We look to the future for something better. . . . We ask and wonder because we have hope that things can be set right and those that are already right can be affirmed."

To these affirmations I say, Amen! The American people, or at least a significant portion of them, have been struggling with increasing frustration to find political and social and moral answers to the contradictions and inadequacies of our society and of our lives. The very frustration that marks so many Americans is itself evidence that we know we can do better than we are now doing. There are in fact better approaches and better solutions and a far wider range of priorities to meet the difficulties and dangers that beset our world than we have yet found.

I believe and I find sustenance in these pages for the belief that the salvation of America lies in a modern-day effort to live by the ancient command to "love your neighbor as yourself"—and to understand as the Good Samaritan did that our neighbor may be next door, on the street, or in a distant foreign land.

Conscientious citizens are driven to look more closely at how their tax dollars are being spent. It is our taxes that help finance hot lunches for school children, food stamps to enhance the nutritional health of the poor, education for the young, and security assistance for the elderly. But taxes also pay for the further accumulation of nuclear weapons long after we have passed the point where, like the Soviets, we could absorb a nuclear strike from the other side and still respond with enough devastating retaliation to destroy much of civilization.

If a fraction of the funds now being poured into useless and dangerous "overkill" for the military could be devoted to human welfare "wonders could be performed" at home and abroad.

And beyond all of these considerations of what we owe to others as a matter of right looms the tested assurance that "whenever you did this for one of the least important of these brothers of mine, you did it for me" (Matthew 25:40).

George McGovern

Introduction

In the early part of 1981, on a New York City TV talk show, a producer appeared to promote her special for television. It was a 60-minute profile of Mother Teresa of Calcutta.

The discussion between the host and the producer necessarily probed into some of the saddest duties of Mother Teresa's daily life. There was talk of leprosy and malnutrition, of poverty and dying in the streets, of the hopelessness of the world's forgotten poor and the horrid conditions they are condemned to exist in.

Throughout the lengthy interview, commercials were interspersed, providing an ironic counterpoint to the memories the producer had:

Lepers (pause) bikinis for sale.
Starvation (pause) designer jeans.
Crying poverty (pause) fur coats.
Abandoned babies (pause) ice cream sundaes.
The dying (pause) diamond watches.

After a spate of ads for oil heat, Krazy Glue, and a furniture store, the producer recalled Mother Teresa's words: "The West is suffocating from muchness."

We have too much; they have too little. We worry about the price of oil heat; they wonder if they will freeze to death tonight. We are dying for an ice cream cone; they are dying.

And during every 60-second commercial, 30 more children died of malnutrition. Every two seconds, someone real slumped in someone's arms and died. Someone with a name and a personality and a gift and a funny way of grinning and an odd birthmark in an odd location and a tendency to stutter on the letter "W" and a sense of humor died, was no more, became null, was erased from the planet.

It is against those contrasts that this book is written. And it is written on the premise that the poor of the world deserve some of our affluence—not because of charity but because of justice. They have a right to what we have. And we must give it to them, not out of kindness or sentiment or big-heartedness, but because it is theirs. It is our obligation to set the balance right, to unskew the line, to re-program the computer, to put the lop-sides straight.

This is not, I repeat, the work of charity. Charity means giving someone something extra, something he or she doesn't really need. Justice is giving someone something he or she needs and deserves, something he or she has a right to.

It is not charity to give an accused person a fair trial. It is justice. (It is charity to give that person a reduced sentence or a chance to reform or a TV in his cell.)

It is not charity to give a hungry person something to eat. It is justice. (It is charity to give that person steak when bread will do or beer when water is all that is needed.)

The purpose of this book is to examine our duty toward the world's needy and our responsibility toward our own affluence. We have something; they have nothing: How do we go about setting that right? Where is the balance point? What do they deserve? What do we need? How can we be more responsible with our blessings? What can we justly keep for ourselves? How do we handle our wealth?

Throughout these pages, two groups are kept in mind—those with and those without (the haves and have-nots). The former have a responsibility toward the latter; that is one consideration. But the former also have a responsibility toward themselves; that is another theme. We cannot help others until we have set our own houses in order, until we have come to some philosophy of affluence, until we have decided how we want to live, until we set some goals.

In making these points, I have tried to avoid giving sample figures. I did this for two reasons: 1. Each person's case is different, and there is no way to set down dummy cases which will cover everyone's situation; 2. The world changes rapidly. In a book published in 1964, for example, the author wrote:

"Your occupational group will automatically set certain limits on your earning potential. If you drive a taxi, you can expect to earn between $3,500 and $6,000 a year; you will never make $15,000 or live in a $30,000 house. If you are a physician, you should expect to make between $10,000 and $30,000. . . . (There is a) slow but sure inflation, boosting the cost of living about 3 percent a year."

The same book estimated that the average family of five spends $65 a month for housing and $170 a month for food.

Taxi drivers now earn what doctors used to and live in homes they never dreamed of in 1964.

Things change. To avoid such dating and to evade giving specific examples (to which the reader is too often tempted to say, "That's not my situation"), I have tried to remain more general. Doing so demands more of the reader who must apply the suggestions to his or her own case, making the necessary adjustments and applying the general guidelines to the particular circumstances of life.

Finally, every reader has the right to ask of the author, "Who does he think he is? Where does he get off telling me this?"

I think I am no different from most of the people reading this book. A wage earner with a wife and three kids, I know the pressures of living today. But I also know that those pressures don't excuse me from considering the plight of the people who have no pressures because they have nothing at all.

This book represents my thinking about this topic. I do not hold myself up as a model or saint who is to be imitated—because I am not. In exploring my own finances, I found a great deal lacking in how just I was to the poor. But that is the purpose of the book—to get us to look at ourselves and decide what we can do for the less fortunate.

The first step: let's look at ourselves.

1
The Good Life and Us

All through high school, I was friends with Douglas Kenney. He and I shared several common traits—a healthy disregard for gym class, for example, and a love for Steve Allen's puns. And we were both oriented toward writing. We worked together on the school newspaper, yearbook, and literary annual.

Doug was funnier than I, however. He was constantly coming up with *mots* much more *bon* than mine. It was he, for instance, who once raised his hand in math class when he was puzzled over a logarithm problem. "Would you explain that again," he asked the teacher, "for those of me who don't understand?"

He coupled with his writing ability a flair for drawing and produced cartoons which lampooned his fellow students. "Lampoon," in fact, would become a key word in his life.

After graduating from high school, we split apart, I staying at home to go to college, he traveling to Harvard. There he joined the staff of the famous satire magazine, *The Harvard Lampoon.* Now and again, the local newspapers or the alumni journal would carry some news note about Doug. So from a distance I followed his progress. He graduated from Harvard, went on to found the enormously popular *National Lampoon* magazine, appeared on a couple of TV shows, sold his interest in the magazine for a million dollars or so (when you get up to the first million the "or so" doesn't really matter), and wrote the box-office sensation "Animal House." In turn, that success spun off a short-lived TV series, which he co-authored, and another film, "Caddyshack."

I was in direct contact with Doug only once after high school. I submitted an article to him at the *Lampoon,* and he rejected it with a friendly note and an invitation to try again.

Through all of this, I admit, there was a tinge of jealousy on my part. Big bucks, Hollywood, success—they seemed like goals worth racing after, and Doug had not only entered the chase, he had won.

And then I came across the most recent clipping about my high school friend. I was paging through the daily newspaper, reading the small items used to fill space when the advertising falls short. A headline caught my eye: "'Animal House' writer found dead."

Doug's body had been found at the bottom of a cliff in Hawaii. He had been missing several days before police came across his remains. At the age of 34, he was dead. And, at the age of 34, I was no longer jealous.

No one knows whether he slipped off the edge of the cliff or jumped or was pushed. It doesn't really make any difference. What does matter is that he was dead, and his bank accounts, movie contracts, TV residuals, and fame would not restore him to life.

Doug was affluent to me. To someone in Zambia, I am affluent. And, undoubtedly, there are tribes somewhere in the interior of Zambia who think the farmer on the coast is a wealthy man because he makes $300 a year and has land to till. But Doug, I, the farmer, and the tribesman should know what we have in common—not the level of our affluence but the responsibility to use that affluence properly so that when we are called to account we don't have to stammer a weak response.

My words are not directed, of course, to the Zambian farmer. Nor are they intended for the Appalachian coal-miner who is out of work or the welfare mother or the man who sleeps under cardboard beneath the railroad over-pass. They are intended for the vast number of people who earn a living in America, whether they bring home a small paycheck or tote up their perquisites with the help of a tax attorney. The former designation includes me; the latter included Doug. For us and everyone in between, I intend these words about the use of affluence.

"Money makes the world go around," declares the cynical song in "Cabaret," disputing the more romantic notion that "Love makes the world go around." And it sometimes seems that indeed our lives are driven madly by a mechanism whose cogs are shaped like dollar signs.

"Buy a new one," we say when something malfunctions.

"That's more expensive than this one; it must be better," we tell our spouses when shopping.

"How much did it cost?" we ask a neighbor who is displaying a new purchase. Never mind how it works, why it was needed, and where it came from—we want to know its price tag.

Bigger is better, more expensive is better. Buy on time, but buy. Get a raise and prove your worth. We are judged by our bank accounts and the visible signs of its size: homes, cars, electronic geegaws, our children's clothing, our wife's new coat, our husband's new golf clubs (and, so as to avoid sexism, our wife's new tennis racket and our husband's new sports outfit).

One day recently, my son was preparing for his nightly

bath in the usual manner—by shedding his clothing willy-nilly around the house, leaving evidence of his passing much like a snake whose skin is sloughing off. My daughter, barely past her second birthday, pounced on one particular pile of clothing, pointed gleefully and began shouting an incomprehensible (to me) chant.

"Hay-mah, hay-mah," she repeated again and again, her finger touching the label on the clothing.

My wife laughed, "Don't you hear what she's saying?" She picked up the clothing and brought it to me. "Read the label."

"K-Mart," I said, my eyes brightening.

"Hay-mah," my daughter repeated after me, happy in the knowledge that her father had connected with her.

My child, just past two, had recognized and correctly identified the corporate logo of a supermart, and she delighted in her recognition. She is the same child who walks with the family to communion and wears a sadly puzzled expression because she cannot figure out what we are eating and why she is excluded from the repast.

My daughter knows K-Mart but not Jesus. And I think she might represent a lot of us. We know how much a Granada costs but not how to pray. We can list the best brands of wine but not the best saints to admire. We can expound on the intricacies of bank accounts, charge cards, and retirement plans but go dumb when asked what the church teaches about money. In other words, we have chosen to wallow in the world which spins because of money. We have hopped happily aboard the lucre-go-round.

We live in a society dominated by money and the pursuit of it. To live there does not mean we have to love it—but most of us do. We glory in the billboards which display a shapely derriere modeling designer jeans autographed by a fictional character created in some corporate headquarters. We eagerly lap up TV commercials for diet beer. We daily peruse newspaper ads which proffer their goodies before our eyes. We page quickly through magazines, searching for the latest in this and the best in that. Stores lure us into their dens with promises of bargains and more bargains, sales on top of sales, and specials unheard of in history. Products beckon us with vows to make our lives simpler, easier, more comfortable, less harried, less complicated, fuller, sweeter, happier.

Take any magazine and flip through, paying attention to the ads. What are they telling us? I grabbed a copy of staid old *Time* and it told me this:

- Oldsmobile "had one built for" me;
- "Nobody does it better" than Winston Lights;
- The taste of Bailey's Irish cream liqueur is "magic";
- "Nothing else feels like real gold";
- Puerto Rican rums taste like nothing else;
- Tareyton cigarettes are smooth, distinctive, and safer;
- Old Grand-Dad bourbon is "rich-tasting";
- Seville is "the ultimate American motor car";
- "Save 20 percent at Sears";
- Republic Airlines is convenient and goes anywhere I'm going.

That's just a handful of ads from one magazine for one week. Read again the adjectives used. Pick up an issue for yourself and check the photos—they speak volumes more than the copy. Drink their wine and blondes will lie beside you. Smoke this cigarette and you'll be a rough-tough cowpoke. Drive that car and you'll be a racecar driver at the Indianapolis 500. Safe, ultimate, rich, the best.

And all that effort was expended on things we don't need—smokes, wines, liquors, fancy cars—but which we buy because we are affluent. The evidence shows that, in spite of all the worry about inflation, unemployment, and other economic woes, we still live in an affluent society where the majority of people are warm, well-fed, educated, safe, and free.

We are affluent. Our nation abounds with goodies both material and intangible. Many natural resources exist in large supply, and what we don't have we can buy from someone else. Freedom, though sometimes threatened, is our foundation. We can cross state borders without facing guard dogs and roadblocks; we can go to church without losing our jobs; we can read and write what we want without having the former confiscated and the latter censored; we can gather in a town square and speak against the local powers without being placed in jail the next morning.

While a pessimist would argue that American industry daily pumps out pollution and poison, I would counter that it also pumps out shoes for our kids, TVs for our rec rooms, appliances for the kitchen, gizmos for our merriment, and Krazy Glue. The pessimist would rant against the medical establishment, listing fee splitting and other unethical practices as some of the charges to be leveled. But that same establishment saves our lives with wonder drugs, researches and conquers disease, eases our pain, prolongs our life span, and turns our children into better physical beings than we were at their age.

Government, industry, medicine, the church—it's easy to rip them and to find flaws. I'm not denying those flaws, but I am reminding us of their achievements. And those achievements add up to a national affluence unparalleled in human history.

To be blunt: we have it pretty good.

I can hear a voice from the rear of the room saying, "Doesn't this guy buy gas? Doesn't he see his salary shrink with inflation and his take-home pay diminish with taxes? Doesn't he know what the mortgage interest rate is? Hasn't he looked into tuition costs for college? Hasn't he checked the price of milk, meat and medicine?"

The answer in each case is yes; I'm as aware as anyone of the ravages of inflation, the sting of unemployment, the burden of taxation. But I still say we have it pretty good. The obvious comparison is to take our homes—with all the heating bills and mortgage payments—and place them next to a mud hut in Cambodia. The rice farmer who owns that hut doesn't have a mortgage, sees no tax man, needs no oil delivery service, doesn't celebrate Christmas (and so doesn't have Christmas bills in February), doesn't face unemployment since he farms only to feed his family, and couldn't care less about inflation.

Would we care to swap homes with him?

That's the obvious come-back. There are others. For example, for all the whining by some Americans that inflation is eating them up, we still spend—in one single day—$54,794 just to fight drandruff. That's every day of the year.

We Americans who wonder where our tax money is going are the same ones who drink 90 million cans of beer a day. The same men and women who shake their heads over the price of gasoline smoke 1.6 billion cigarettes—every 24 hours.

The Good Life and Us

Things can't be too tough when we still manage to puff while we huff. The slings and arrows of outrageous economies are painful, but we still smoke, drink our brew, and shampoo with lemon-scented suds. Life can't be all that hard when we subscribe to *TV Guide* (despite getting a free one in the paper), buy pantyhose, scarf down Twinkies, go to ballgames, stock up on electric appliances which brush our caps or open our beer cans, purchase hand-held football games and mini-computers, take vacations, put braces on Elmer's teeth, send Bernice to ballet lessons, and plunk down four bucks to see a bad movie while munching dollar-a-bucket popcorn.

If we can still do any one of these things, we are affluent.

As individuals and as a nation, we are affluent. The United States, for all its fits and fights over Vietnam, Watergate, the economy, states' rights, taxation, abortion, equal rights, racism, and a barrelful of other wrenching issues, remains in a united state. In this, we are affluent.

America, running out of oil, remains fat with natural gas and mineral resources and arable land. In these, we are affluent.

Our country serves its citizens—no matter how slothful or unresponsive the bureaucracy—through garbage pick-ups, vast highway systems, welfare programs, and much more. In that, we are affluent.

In its rich texture of ethnic and racial cultures, in its cities and farms, in its communications boom, in its ability to weather storms of all sorts, in its pride and power, our nation is affluent.

I don't want this to turn into a paean to the flag and White House. A great deal is wrong with America. It aborts its unborn and wonders why children are abused, it puts criminals to death and is perplexed that life is held cheaply, it represses its minorities and then castigates them for demanding their rights, it burdens its taxpayers and then is amazed when the common person goes apathetic. But our nation also throbs with those who would redress these wrongs—and that is still another affluence. We are affluent in our energy and brains and stirring desire to fix what's wrong; we are affluent in our system of government, no matter how crazy its functioning.

And in this affluent place, we are affluent people. Each of us is affluent in material possessions, as well as in less tangible ones. Let's look at the former first. Walk through your home and touch everything that marks you as affluent:

—the two TVs, three radios, and stereo;
—the two cars;
—the washer, dryer, dishwasher, mixer, blender, iron;
—the central air conditioning;
—the souvenirs from your vacations;
—the oak table in the living room and glasstop coffee table in the den;
—your cologne, after-shave, electric shaver, and hair blower;
—your perfume, make-up, and portable hair dryer;
—the wall-to-wall carpeting;
—the ticket stubs from a movie or play;
—record albums and tapes;
—magazines, books, newspapers;
—the shoes in the closet, including the pairs you never wear;
—the monogrammed ties, sweaters, and pajamas;

—the country club membership;
—the power mower and snow blower;
—the Princess phone.

We may not have them all, but if we have one of them we are affluent. Each one represents something we could get along without. In place of our cars, our feet; instead of air conditioning, an open window; no record albums, just our voices; no shoes, just sore toes.

The bills for these things may be sky-high, we may be in debt, we may shake our heads over how much they cost—but we still have them and then buy more, all because we are affluent.

Pause for a moment right now and jot down some of your possessions, things which mark you as affluent.

How many of them do you still owe on? How many of them do you really need (not want, need)? Could you get along without them? What if they disappeared tomorrow—would you be devastated and unable to function? I doubt it. Think about it a moment. If your TVs, radios, stereos, and electronic games stopped working, would you fold into a jellied mass of inactivity? Life might become more inconvenient if your car wouldn't start or your washing machine died, but would their absence ruin your existence?

I don't think so. Time and again, men and women have proved their resilience, their ability to adapt to any circumstance. A natural disaster will occur (or even a simple power outage), the amenities of life are removed—and people still get by. In fact, they seem to flourish. People who face tough times often comment that those were the happiest times of their lives.

That ability to adapt and flourish, I submit, is but one more sign that we are affluent. If we can get along without such possessions, then they must be, in the final analysis, superfluous. And people who possess superfluous things are called affluent.

Perhaps our affluence doesn't match that of the tycoon who owns six Rolls Royces and homes in Hawaii, Capri, and the Greek isles, but we are affluent. Maybe our affluence can't stack up against that of the woman who dines on caviar, flies to Paris for the latest fashions, and owns steel mills in Sweden, but we are affluent. Compared to our friend, the Cambodian farmer, we are the super-rich. Compared to the silver kings of Texas, we are pikers. But looked at objectively, we are affluent. Where we fall on the scale of affluence is varied, but we land on it somewhere.

Only in America, during Christmastime, can you flick on the TV and see ads begging you to buy an electric tooth polisher and an electric egg scrambler. Life can't be too hard when there is a market for a machine that spins an egg in its shell so that Mr. and Mrs. Homemaker don't have to wear out their forearms twirling a spatula. As for that tooth polisher, it comes with the suggestion that purchasers order two—one for themselves and one for their dog.

Out of every 1,000 homes in America:

—999 have TV sets;
—999 have refrigerators;
—999 have vacuum cleaners;
—997 have coffeemakers;
—733 have clothes washers;
—599 have electric blankets;

—448 have home freezers;
—409 have dishwashers;
—67 have microwave ovens.

The average Jennifer and Michael of America (those were the two most popular names for white babies born in a recent year) go to five movies a year, listen to 21 hours of radio a week, watch TV (half of the sets in use are color) six hours a day, spend more than $800 on a stereo, take more than 100 snapshots of each other annually, and are overweight.

We are affluent. Period.

In our Master Charge cards, designer jeans, leather jackets, power steering, filtertips, fast food, wine with dinner out, weekends at the shore, color portables, three-piece suits, giant-size boxes of soap powder, time payments, insurance, digital watches, and frozen daiquiri mix, we are affluent.

Folks, we're living pretty good. You and I may be eating lower on the hog, but we still have the hog. And we still have some other possessions, less tangible ones, which mark us as even more affluent than we might think.

Other Affluences

The reason that Americans are sometimes judged to be a trifle screwy is that they are free. Seen from a distant nation, even those older places of liberty, the U.S. sometimes looks like a madhouse. There are civil rights demonstrators being hosed down, gay rightists bussing on the streets, busing opponents chanting, pro-lifers and pro-choicers jostling for network coverage, equal rights advocates making speeches, Nazis and Klanners parading in their costumes. It sometimes looks as if Ringling Bros. had taken over the streets.

But the chaos on the surface and the turmoil which sometimes results are not what Americans should be judged by. They should be judged by what allows them to go into the streets speaking their minds—without the fear of a tank at the other corner, aimed in their direction.

Freedom. Liberty. The Bill of Rights. These are some of the affluences Americans enjoy, take for granted until a crisis occurs (Watergate, the Iranian hostages) and then rally around. Like few other countries in the world, the U.S. allows its citizens freedom—to speak, to write, to demonstrate, to travel, to assemble, to worship.

To go from New Hampshire to Hawaii, you don't need a passport, you don't have to go through checkpoints, you don't have to declare your possessions or allegiance. And when you return home, your family will still be there. You can write an article critical of the government and be asked to write more, not to report to the federal building for deportation. You can harangue people from a soapbox and come back the next day for more—without fear that your soapbox or self will be toted away.

We are free. It's an affluence we seldom think of. Until it is threatened, we take it for granted, so ingrained is it in our consciousness.

Freedom is only one of our intangible affluences. We also enjoy health, opportunity, security, and hope.

Health. Every now and then, statistics will appear deploring the physical condition of Americans. They are fat, prone to heart disease, riddled with tar and nicotine, breeding grounds for cancer. Their children are malnourished from dining on too many potato chips and french fries.

But these, in themselves, are signs of affluence. Our monetary affluence attacks our medical affluence in these cases. With so much money, we squander it on burgers, cigarettes, and diet cola. Diet cola is especially ironic. Our affluence makes us fat so our affiuence allows us to concoct a chemical substance to ingest in hopes of becoming thin again; in turn, the chemical formula turns on us and threatens to give us cancer—so our affluence pays for medical research into cures. It would be ludicrous were it not so tragic.

But health is still an affluence available to us. We are drowning in doctors; medical insurance pays for our operations; dentists perfect their equipment so that pain becomes outmoded; all sorts of notions stock the drugstore shelves, each with the potential to help us in some way—by removing our warts, bandaging our cuts, cleaning our ears, getting us through colds, shrinking our hemorrhoids, banishing the red from our eyes, or silencing our coughs for the night.

Again, compare us with someone far less fortunate. Our medical establishment may have a lot to indict it, but its defense would be strong. I'd hate to have any malady—from a case of the sniffles to an attack of cancer—in some clearing in the woods of Botswana. I'll take my chances here where I can get second opinions, shop around for the best medication, try generic drugs, and check into a hospice.

Opportunity. The all-American dream used to be that any little boy can become President and any little girl can become head nurse. The sexual stereotyping has changed, but the dream is still there—and still can be realized. Think of where recent Presidents have come from. They weren't born on plantations or in palaces. And anyone who wants to be anything can be—if he or she is qualified and capable. No matter your name, religion, race, point of origin, age—no matter anything, you can become what you want to be. And when you're blocked ("Hispanics need not apply"), it's because something is wrong, not because the nation approves of it.

A child born today in America can become a doctor, lawyer, ditch-digger, chemist, computer engineer, sanitary engineer, janitor, left-fielder, ballet star, clerk, cosmetic salesperson, accountant, telephone repairman, bank teller, counselor—am I running on too long?—security guard, steelworker, construction worker, cabbie, painter of landscapes or barnsides, farmer, reporter—I'm nowhere near running out—midwife, tailor, architect, upholsterer, brewer, pilot, lifeguard, firefighter, comedian, landscaper, vet—somebody stop me, please—waiter, politician, blackjack dealer, mortician—I've got to stop.

Take a look at any newspaper's want ads. You'll find companies searching for all sorts of people and the only qualification is that they can do the job. No one is born to soldier or doctor us. No one is picked out at infancy to be a king. There is unlimited opportunity open to everyone. Story after story of American success rides on the opportunity available in this country.

Security. A great deal has been written and said lately about "walking the streets at night" and how dangerous an occupation it is. It's a serious problem. Crime, whether it is in the ghetto or along the suburban avenues, is frightening. It threatens life and property. But we are, nonetheless, a pretty secure people. No stormtroopers break into our homes at night. The police are not our enemies. Roving gangs of pillagers don't wander the cityscapes.

We are, relatively, safe. As for walking the streets at night, I often wonder why people want to. I agree that they should be able to, but this is not Utopia. You couldn't walk the streets at night in Caesar's Rome or Elizabeth's London either.

We are physically safe—and mentally and emotionally safe, too. No one single entity is trying to propagandize us. Lots of entities are—from the government to the butcher down the street. But freedom of speech makes sure that no one's propaganda goes unanswered or unchallenged. The free exchange of ideas keeps us safe from being brainwashed.

Hope. All of the previous affluences give us this most necessary one—hope. We are people of hope. As Christians and Americans (and the two are different, let's remember), we have hope. Hope in our promises from God, hope in our political future, hope in our freedoms, hope in our opportunities, hope in our children.

We have been tested—as both Christians and Americans—and we have come through. We have made it through Vietnam, Watergate, and the Iranian hostages, to name three recent tests. We have not come through unscarred or unblemished; we have not come through without shame and fault. But we have come through, and we have survived to hope for something better in the future.

The ferment in our society, both our religious and political societies, is a sign of our hope. We look to the future for something better. So we agitate and search and question and probe. We wonder why women can't be priests or why nuclear power plants have to be built. We ask why the church does this or the government does that. We ask and wonder because we have hope that things can be set right and those that are already right can be supported.

In our hope, security, opportunity, health, and freedom, we are affluent, just as we are affluent in our material goods. In between these intangibles and tangibles, there is one more affluence—our natural resources. We are abundantly blessed with water, air, trees, crops, fertile soil, energy sources, spectacular natural wonders, and space. We are not crammed into a corner of another nation; we are not landlocked; we do not thirst every drought season; we do not wonder if we will have a harvest every fall. We have all that we need and more.

We are affluent.

In our material wealth.

In our resources.

In our hope, opportunities, freedoms, health, and security.

We are affluent in all of these.

We are materially affluent, and those who are not have the opportunity to become so. We are blessed with natural resources, and those we don't have we can trade for from our abundance. We have stockpiled high our stores of liberty and security. We are rich in health.

We are so blessed, rich, and affluent that we sometimes forget that there are people—down the block, in the neighboring state, around the world—who are not like us.

2
The People in the Basement

Kapila Nayer, an eight-year-old, pig-tailed girl from New Delhi, is not like us. When she was asked what the purpose of America's Thanksgiving Day was, she replied, "It is when Americans pray to their gods because they got so rich."

Her brother offered the opinion that those riches allowed Americans to enjoy "plenty of sweets and TV games."

Christina Longhi, a 12-year-old Italian, is not like us. To her, Thanksgiving is when Americans "thank God for living so well. They eat a lot of food."

Lin Yuyi, of Peking, is not like us. To Lin, Americans are a race of people "who ride around in their motor cars and eat steak."

Riches, sweets, TV games, cars, and steaks: these are America to those who live in other parts of the world. Their choices are as American as apple pie—with ice cream on top after a full dinner of turkey with gravy and dressing, followed by a football game viewed on a 19-inch color set.

It's easy, when asked to compare our affluence with others', for us to compare upwards. Turn to any sports section in the nation and you'll read angry letters from fans protesting the salaries paid to baseball players and other heroes of the turf. Dave Winfield, it is pointed out, makes $170 an hour—year round, whether he plays or not, 24 hours a day. Every time he hits the ball, another thousand or so clinks into his money belt.

There is more than affluence in the U.S. There is also luxury. Writing in *Time* magazine, Roger Rosenblatt commented that "on any given street on a given day, Rolls-Royces idle bumper to splendid bumper; the air is soaked in Bal a Versailles; diamonds go like Tic Tacs. From now to Christmas, *The New Yorker* will be heavy with ads for crystal yaks and other lavish doodads in 'limited editions,' for which one assumes there must be buyers. Saks Fifth Avenue, which advertises itself as all the things we are, has recently decided that we are a 14-karat gold charge plate ($750). . . . David Bowie, the rock star, outfitted his Lincoln Continental with a television, paintings, and plants hanging from the roof. And a Saudi sheik recently bought a jet that he furnished with a $40,000 mink bedspread and 24-karat gold shower fixtures."

Reading such things as these, ordinary people often excuse themselves from justice. We are the poor, we declare in face of such extravagance by the super-rich. They have the diamonds; we have the Tic Tacs. In so saying, we forget those who have only the ticks.

When someone else has a Rolls, our Chevette seems terribly tacky—and never mind those who have to walk. When rock stars and baseball players are dining on caviar, we consider our meatloaf a sign of abject poverty. How then can we turn to help those who lunch on handfuls of rice and tree bark?

But luxury does not excuse us. It may outshine but it does not bury our affluence. We must compare in the other direction; we must turn our eyes from those above us and gaze at those behind us. It's not easy to do. It's easier to look at the half dozen sheiks in front of us than the half billion gaunt figures in back of us. But we were not placed on earth to do the easy things.

And the fact that some things are hard for us doesn't free us from our responsibility toward those in need. It may be difficult to scrape together enough for a down payment on a better home, but it's far easier than having to scrape together enough to feed your starving children. Getting the mortgage money is different from getting out of the slums. Moving up is different from moving out of poverty. Affluence is different from subsisting.

Sixty percent of the people of the world consume less than the minimum 2200 calories a day needed to maintain health. About 50 percent of the world's people earn less than $100 a year. As Yvonne Goulet, writing in *U.S. Catholic* put it, "Against these statistics, the relentless acquisition of Americans is obscene." Against statistics such as those, we are rock stars, ball players, and sheiks. Against statistics like those, we are a people of candy and TVs, steaks, and Pintos.

In a year in which Americans complained about their annual inflation rate of 13 percent, Israel and Brazil were two nations with inflation rates over 110 percent. In that same year, some nations had no inflation rate because they had nothing to inflate. If you don't earn $100 a year, it doesn't make much difference how much they inflate the currency. You can raise the price of gasoline, chicken breasts, handheld computers, and two-doors all you want as far as the people of such nations are concerned.

And, unless we do something, the plight of such people will only get worse. "Global 2000," a report filed by the

State Department and the Council on Environmental Quality, looked at present trends in world production and consumption, and arrived at some terrifying conclusions.

In parts of the Mideast, Africa, and Asia, "the quantity of food available to the poorest groups will simply be insufficient to permit children to reach normal body weight and intelligence." While the U.S. continues to munch on the fruits of its abundance, millions will be dying or suffering, doomed to deficiency—mental and physical—because of our insensitivity, because of our lack of justice toward them.

That same report predicts a more crowded, more polluted, less safe, and disturbingly different world unless we do something. Water shortages will occur more frequently; between 500,000 and two million species of animal, insect, and plant life will become extinct, wiped off the face of the earth forever because of pollution and urban sprawl; increasing air toxicity will affect the climates, changing rich lands into arid wastes.

It will happen, unless we, the more affluent, do something.

Imagine for a moment a large mansion. In it live 100 people. On the upper three floors, 30 people live in rooms heated in the winter and air conditioned in the summer. There is a bathroom for every five of them and a bedroom for each person. The children have private tutors; the adults have access to TVs, stereos, radios, and a library; the elderly are cared for by nurses.

The other 70 (and you are among them in this story) live in the cellar in a cramped corner. The dirt floor is your bed. You share the windowless existence with rats and spiders. Instead of a bathroom, the 70 of you share two buckets. Occasionally, when they are done with them, the 30 above you will throw down some things—a blanket here, an old shirt there. Every now and then, especially when one of your children gets sick, they will roll an aspirin down the stairs.

Every day the 100 of you order food to be delivered. Sometimes, 100 hamburgers; sometimes, 100 pizzas. But every time the deliveryman comes, he leaves 90 of the burgers or pizzas upstairs and brings only 10 to the cellar. Thirty people above are living on 90 burgers, while 70 below have to make do with 10.

Things, in short, are out of whack in this house. If you were one of the cellar-dwelling 70, what would you do? Would you suffer in silence? Would you say the upper 30 were just luckier? Would you try to do something? Would you start up the stairs? Would you ambush the deliveryman? Would you begin fashioning weapons for an attack on the library? Would you plead for the teachers and nurses to come down at least once in a while? Would you wonder why the higher 30 needed so many pizzas for so few and why they didn't send their surplus downstairs?

What would you do?

The house, of course, is our world and it is out of whack, too. Two-thirds of the world's population lives in poverty, huddled in shacks, dining on scraps, ekeing out a meager existence. Their children are naked, uneducated, and hungry. Those who make it to old age have nothing to remember; the young have nothing to hope for. This two-thirds, the ones in the cellar of the world, is oppressed physically, emotionally, and spiritually. And the people upstairs—which is where *we* live in reality—are not doing enough for them; we are not being just to them. It is their right to have enough to eat, enough to wear, a place to live, education, opportunity, health, security, and hope.

Consider the affluences we have and contrast our lives with theirs:

Material affluence. Two-thirds of the world earns, in essence, nothing. What they have, they barter for or build themselves. In India, part of Mother Teresa's Nobel Prize money went to build houses for the poor. The cost per house: $125. You won't find TV antennas on the roofs of hovels in Brazil or Hondas in the driveways of shacks in Thailand. But these people are not looking for TVs and cars; they are looking for possessions far less grandiose: clothing, cooking utensils, books, medicine.

Health. In those photos of starving children which circulate in the news magazines whenever there is a lull in the opera season or a lack of public relations puffery from Hollywood, the dominant image is of distended stomachs and matchstick limbs. Such people are in the final stages of hunger; they are ready to die. Born in poverty, they have lived in poverty, and will die the same. Born in sickness, they grew up in illness, and will die from one malady or another. The poor are prone to illness; defenseless because they are malnourished, they are prey to all sorts of diseases. Leprosy, tuberculosis, diphtheria: they crawl in the villages of the poor. A child without food is a child ready to become sick.

A simple illness, which the affluent can pass off with two days in bed and some drugstore medication, will kill a poor person. While Americans pop Valiums by the handsful, spend five times as much for brand-name aspirin (when they could have the same product for less under a generic label) and have access to doctors, dentists, midwives, nurses, counselors and all sorts of medical personnel, the cellar-dwellers of the world lie in fevers and chills.

Security. What security can there be for a poor person? True, they have nothing to hand a thief, but they have plenty to give to the thief called the present—namely, their lives. Remember the Vietnamese boat people? They were the most pitiful of refugees, huddled on boats, trying to find freedom. Yet they were the target of pillage and rape and slavers.

They have no way of protecting themselves and no one to turn to for help. At the mercy of everyone and every quirk of nature, the poor huddle against each other in hopes they will survive the night.

Opportunity. Why don't the poor get a job? Why don't they get some ambition? Why do they want a handout?

Every one of us has asked those questions. But we seldom stay for the answers. We don't want to hear that there are no jobs or that the jobs they do have pay them annually what we bring home after a few days of work. We don't want to know that starvation kills ambition, that those seeking to keep alive have little time to seek employment, that children born of poverty and reared in despair have no knowledge of ambition, that lack of food kills the spirit as well as the body. As for handouts, we never want to listen to the distinction between charity and justice. We can deny a handout or feel peacock proud when we give one; but to hear about justice and rights is too much.

The only opportunity the poor have is the opportunity to remain poor. There are no Horatio Alger stories in Calcutta.

Hope. Hope is concerned with the future. The poor have no future.

A poor person hopes he can apportion the rice to his children without killing himself. A poor person hopes she can suckle her baby from a desiccated breast. A poor person hopes death will come quietly and quickly.

It is not right or just that people live that way. These people have a right to what we have; they have a right to our surplus; they have a right to our affluence; they have a right to demand that the blessings which the deliveryman has given us be passed down to them. They have a right to equality. They have a right to demand from us what we have not given.

No matter what woes befall us, chances are that they are nowhere near the tragedies that strike at the people in the world's cellar. Americans tend to see visions of Armageddon every time they tear their pantyhose, crease their rocker panel, burn out their lawn, or break a picture window. Even the more desperate situations facing some of us—unemployment, for example, or the inability to sock away some savings—are nothing compared to the tragedies facing the majority of the world's peoples.

Yes, there are tragedies in America. Yes, even the affluent are afflicted in ways that money cannot cure. But when such things occur, they are aberrations, not the stuff of everyday life. The child dead of Sudden Infant Death Syndrome is tragic, but that baby is the exception. The corpses of the infants of Sahel are not exceptions; they are the rule.

The worries of our lives should not be trivial. We should not be concerned with how to spend our next paycheck (will I buy chicken or ground beef?) when there are people concerned with how long through the night they will hear their child's breathing. In other words, we must see life on a grander scale than we do now. The house of the world must be thought about, not just the houses on our block.

Those living in luxury do not excuse us from being just to the poor. Our own problems do not allow us to forget those whose problems are worse. That there is one man living in a castle and eating a thousand burgers alone does not permit the 30 upstairs to grab all they can. That the 30 upstairs have to paint the walls and scrub the floors does not excuse them from looking in the cellar. That those in the cellar do not help themselves does not give us a reason to slam the door at the head of the stairs.

"Let the people of India take care of the starving of Calcutta" is a convenient alibi, but it does not wash. We can urge the Indians to take care of their own, we can wonder why that government doesn't do more, we can puzzle over their failures and flaws. But we cannot stop there because our wondering, puzzling, and urging won't feed the hungry or heal the sick.

The house of the world contains all sorts of people, and they are all interrelated. Some have odd shadings to their skin (they are called white); some have strange accents (probably Americans); others have different religious practices (Roman Catholics?)—but they all have in common their kinship in Christ.

Who is my neighbor? Jesus was asked. He replied with the story of the Good Samaritan. Our neighbors are everyone everywhere, and our response to them should be compassion and aid. The Samaritan gave from his affluence to help someone who would have been labeled an enemy. The Samaritan did not withhold his goods because of the wounded man's color or political ideology or stench.

He gave because the man was in need; that was the only criterion needed.

The two great commandments, Jesus explained clearly, are love of God and love of neighbor. Too many of us spend our time doing the former while skillfully avoiding the latter or limiting our love to those neighbors we feel comfortable with. But Jesus supped with sinners, prostitutes, sell-outs, drunkards, liars, cheats, sharpies. His purpose was to bring them to God through forgiveness and love. We can bring the poor of the world to God through our love and through justice. They have not sinned by being born in Bangladesh or by contracting tuberculosis or by living in a wasteland without water or arable land. They don't seek forgiveness; they seek and deserve justice.

Those in the cellar are looking up the stairs and wondering why no one comes down. The time may come when they will go up and take what they rightly deserve.

"How can we be indifferent to the millions and millions who live on the brink of starvation each year," asked evangelist Billy Graham, "while the nations of the world spend $550 billion each year on weapons?"

"It is impossible," declared Archbishop Helder Camara of Brazil, "for Christians and for all believers in God and for all persons of good will to support a social order that is above all a social disorder."

The call of Christ and of his church is to remedy that disorder.

3
What Did Jesus Say?

You will have the poor with you forever.

Jesus' realistic statement to Judas has often been quoted by people to justify not doing much for the needy. But that isn't what he meant. He was not saying, "There will always be poor people—so why bother helping them?" He was saying that he would not live much longer and those who loved him should spend what moments they could with him. The poor, whom they should help, would be around after his death; then his followers could reach out to them in his name.

The Scriptures are filled with lessons on justice toward the poor, the use of affluence and the dangers of wealth. With those as a basis, the church has made pronouncements through the 2,000 years of its history on such matters as private property, charity and justice, the rights of the poor to a decent life, and the threat of materialism.

Through these biblical and church teachings, we have a solid basis on which to build our own understanding of justice toward the poor and the use of affluence. The formation of conscience does not occur through osmosis or divine intervention; it occurs through education, thought, and prayer. The latter two each individual must supply on his or her own. The first can be found externally.

For that purpose, what follows are some selected passages from the New Testament and from papal pronouncements. They are presented as guidelines and as starting points for thought and prayer. Some may appeal more than others to each individual, depending on the circumstances of the reader. But, taken together at once or in stages, they constitute a powerful testimony of Christianity on behalf of justice toward the needy.

From the New Testament

1. *The Beatitudes:*

In the Beatitudes, Jesus summarizes, in aphorisms, his teaching on wealth and poverty. In contrasting remarks, he clearly states the difference between those who have and those who have not.

"How happy are you who are poor," he begins; "yours is the kingdom of God. Happy you who are hungry now; you shall be satisfied. Happy you who weep now; you shall laugh." (Luke 6:20–21)

Against that happiness, he places these warnings:

"Alas for you who are rich; you are having your consolation now. Alas for you who have your fill now; you shall go hungry. Alas for you who laugh now; you shall mourn and weep." (Luke 6:24–25)

In those brief sentences, Jesus gives the contrast between the rich and poor. Those who have now will have not later. Those who have not now will have later. It is a reversal he speaks of often, most commonly remembered in the one-liner about the first being last. Those who are proud will be humbled while the humble will gain a place of prominence.

The affluent, he is saying, will one day (on judgment day) know what the poor have suffered while the poor will enjoy surfeit.

It seems pretty cut and dried. Is there anything the affluent can do to avoid the fate that awaits them in eternity? Or are they doomed by their wealth to suffer hunger and woe everlasting? Is Jesus saying that wealth itself is a sin? Is it un-Christian to have a large bank account? Are those who have luxuries automatically damned?

Conversely, are the poor automatically saved? Is it a virtue to be needy? Is it the height of Christian achievement to be born in a hut? Is it better to be without?

The evidence of Jesus' own birth, life, and teachings is powerful. His birthplace was a stable; his hometown was a backwater; his father was a blue-collar worker; his possessions were a cloak and sandals. By living such a life, was Jesus saying that wealth corrupts?

For the answers, he provided other teachings and parables.

2. *The rich young man:*

One can imagine the eager young man who followed Jesus, listening to his words, taking in all the lessons on forgiveness and love. Was he the scion of a shipping family or the descendant of some grandfather wise enough to cast his lot with the right merchants? Perhaps his wealth came to him through good luck or his own perseverance. He may have been a whiz at borrowing and lending. Whatever the source of his income, he was rich.

But he felt a lack in his life. Something was missing. The house with its mosaics didn't satisfy him; the trips to Capri and Athens didn't soothe him; the collection of Egyptian papyri couldn't please him. There was something more he needed, something he couldn't buy in the marketplace, some ache which reminded him that this life was fleeting.

So one day he got the courage to ask Jesus, who seemed to have the secret answer. This poor man from Nazareth had no inner ache because he had found the key. What was it? What, he asked Jesus, do I have to do to possess eternal life?

Keep the commandments, Jesus replied.

But I already do that, the man answered. And still I am not satisfied.

Jesus recognized someone ready for a bigger step. The young man had kept the laws, the do-nots of life. Yet he realized that it was not enough. He was ready for another step on the road to spiritual maturity. That maturity always involves denial, Jesus knew from his own days in the desert. To grow in God's love, one must cast off things. For Jesus, it had been one thing; for this young man, it would be another.

If you want to be perfect, Jesus began, searching the questioner's eyes for a sign of assent, sell what you own. Give the proceeds to the poor. Then follow me.

The young man's smile faded. The secret was now known, and he realized he could never follow it.

The story of the rich young man (Matthew 19: 16–22) gives many of the answers to the questions raised by the Beatitudes. Perfection lies in stripping ourselves of wealth and sharing it with the poor. It is not wealth that condemns us, but the excessive love of wealth and the use of it for selfish purposes.

That is clear from what immediately follows the story of the rich young man.

3. *Camels and the wealthy:*

As Jesus watched the rich young man walk away, shaking his head, he said to his followers, "It's easier for a camel to squeeze through the eye of a needle than for a rich man to get into heaven."

Scripture scholars still debate how large that needle's eye is. Some hold that Jesus was speaking literally, referring to the tiny hole at the top of a needle. Others say that he was making a reference to one of the gates into Jerusalem. Because it was a small gate, it was nicknamed "The Eye of the Needle." A loaded-down camel often had to hunch down to get through while his driver coaxed and yanked.

Needless to say, the wealthy prefer the latter interpretation.

Either way, Jesus was reiterating a point he makes often: possessions hamper people from coming to God. It was a startling point to make, one that left his disciples "astonished." They had always assumed that the rich were the likeliest candidates for salvation. If the wealthy were now being excluded, what chance did they have?

It's a feeling which has lasted even into our own time. It has always been assumed that riches are a sign of God's favor. If a person is good, God will reward that goodness. Anyone who listens to the so-called electronic preachers gets the same message. Their guests are always successful businessmen and singers with hit records. Spiffy clean and dressed impeccably, these people present an outward appearance which must reflect their inner life. Like their clothes and hair, their souls must be impeccable and in control.

Abraham Lincoln's joke that God must like poor people because he made so many of them has never been accepted. On the contrary, it is assumed that God hates poor people. Why else would he banish them to miserable places to live out their decrepit existences? If God likes someone, he or she will end up eating lark's tongues and drinking mead. That this impression is totally at odds with what Jesus taught is never considered. God's favor on the good is interpreted as material favor, not spiritual contentment.

But Jesus shocked his followers by saying the opposite. It is the Apostles who are rich in the things that matter, not the wealthy young man. Matthew is clear. He quotes Peter: "Lord, we have left everything for you. Fishing nets are rotting. Farms are fallow. Our homes are miles away. What about us?"

"Everyone who has left houses, brothers, sisters, father, mother, children or land for the sake of my name will be repaid a hundred times over and also inherit eternal life," Jesus answered. "Many who are first will be last. And the last, first."

4. *Building barns:*

A man (one imagines a whine in his voice) accosted Jesus one time and demanded that he tell the man's brother to hand over half of their inheritance. Jesus refused. I've got nothing to do with that, he said. Since when am I the judge of your claims? You're too worried about your money. You won't be happy even when you get it.

To explain why not, Jesus told a story about a rich landowner whose harvest yielded more than his storage barns could hold. He was in a panic; what was he to do? He couldn't let the crops rot in the fields. The solution: tear down the existing barns and build new, larger ones. Then he could store everything in them and settle back, secure, fat, and happy.

"But God said to him, 'Fool! This very night the demand

will be made for your soul. And this hoard of yours, whose will it be then?' So it is when a man stores up treasure for himself in place of making himself rich in the sight of God." (Luke 12: 13–21)

Wealth brought the landowner only worry and greed. He never had enough. His original barns, built to house what he needed, could not hold what he wanted. So he made storage space for what he wanted. He went from affluence to luxury. His treasures were material and so his life was not spiritual.

The affluent often reduce life to the material. That is their temptation. They are so centered on "things," that they forget the immaterial. Worried about their clothes, they forget their souls; distressed about the temperature of the wine they drink, they ignore any spiritual sustenance; concerned about how many TVs they have, they never look inside themselves to see what drama is playing there.

The story in Luke continues with Jesus urging the disciples not to worry about things, "about your life and what you are to eat, nor about your body and how you are to clothe it. Life means more than food and the body more than clothing."

If God takes care of birds and flowers so that they don't worry, how much more will he make sure that humans are taken care of? It is a question the affluent don't think about. Nor do they think that perhaps the reason God made them affluent was so they could pass it on to the less fortunate. In that way, God can feed and clothe everyone. When the affluent fail to share, they thwart God's plan.

That plan, as the parable of the talents explains, is to have everyone contribute what they can to the good of all.

5. *Investing and sharing:*

The parable of the talents (Matthew 25: 14–30) is not primarily concerned with affluence and the poor. It is one in a series of stories Jesus tells to describe the coming judgment of humankind. But in this instance he uses a monetary symbol—the talent, a denomination of currency—which can be instructive.

Just as the people in the household of the earth are scattered on different floors, so the money in the parable is given in different degrees. One servant gets five, another receives two and the last is given one. Then the master leaves. Upon his return, the first two servants hand him double his investment while the cowardly third man gives back only the original coin, which he had hidden for fear of losing it.

The master took the coin and gave it to the first servant and then threw the emptyhanded one out of the house.

It sounds like a parable on wealth and poverty as written by a corporate board. The rich get richer, the poor get tossed out. In fact, it is a lesson on how people will be judged according to how well they have developed what gifts they have been given. If they take their blessings, no matter how large, and use them for good, they will be rewarded. If they take those blessings and hide them (hoard them, keep them), they will be punished.

If affluence is the blessing, then it must be used properly. Jesus is not giving a seminar in stocks and bonds and how to double your bucks. He is talking about making good and proper use of what we have. And from other words of his, we know that the proper use of wealth is to give it away.

In other words, we will be judged according to how we

have used our affluence. If we misuse it by storing it up in bigger barns (bank accounts, material possessions), we will be judged harshly. If we use it well (sell what you have and give it to the poor), we will be invited into God's sight.

6. *The beggar outside:*

What is the right use of wealth?

To answer, Jesus told the story of the rich man who dressed well and feasted every night. (Luke 16: 19-31) Outside his house, a beggar named Lazarus lay in the road. He was diseased and crippled, and all he wanted was to eat the left-overs of the rich man's feast. Scraps, garbage, crumbs; Lazarus would have settled for them.

The two men died on the same day and the rich man found himself in hell, burned by fire. In heaven, he could see Lazarus, happy, at peace, whole, contented.

"I am in agony here," the rich man called out. "Just dip your finger in water and touch my tongue. A little drop of moisture is all I need, Lazarus."

But Lazarus could not come even if he wanted to, explained Abraham from heaven. A gulf separates heaven from hell. Now Lazarus enjoys all the good things he missed during life, while the rich man, who had his days of luxury and pleasure, knows only what Lazarus knew during his time on earth.

The rich man begged for Abraham to send Lazarus to earth again, to tell the rich man's five brothers about their duties toward the poor, and to warn them not to ignore the beggars at their gates.

But Lazarus was not sent back. If your brothers won't believe Moses and the prophets, Abraham said, why would they believe Lazarus?

The right use of money, Jesus is saying, is to share it with those in need. Earlier in the same part of the Gospel of Luke (16: 9–13), he makes the point even more clearly.

7. *Two masters:*

In one of Jesus' clearest statements on affluence and the duties of those blessed with money, he said this:

"Use money, tainted as it is, to win you friends, and thus make sure that, when it fails you, they will welcome you into the tents of eternity. . . . If you cannot be trusted with money, that tainted thing, who will trust you with genuine riches? . . . No servant can be the slave of two masters; he will either hate the first and love the second, or treat the first with respect and the second with scorn.

"You cannot be the slave both of God and of money."

It is the choice of the affluent: God or money. The feast inside or the beggar at the gate.

Abraham says he cannot send Lazarus back to earth to warn the five rich brothers. If the brothers won't listen to Scripture, they won't listen to Lazarus.

The affluent today have both: Scriptures and Lazarus. We have not only Moses and the prophets but also the words of Jesus. We also have the countless Lazaruses who live in the cellar of the world, longing for some scraps from our table.

What do we owe today's Lazaruses? Just scraps and left-overs? One answer is provided in the example of the early church.

8. *Sharing:*

The early church, led by and in imitation of the Apostles, was made up of people who gave away what they had.

They knew Jesus' words to the rich young man, and they chose to sell what they had rather than to walk away sadly.

As recorded in Acts (4: 32–35), "no one claimed for his own use anything that he had, as everything they owned was held in common. . . . None of their members was ever in want, as all those who owned land or houses would sell them and bring the money from them to present it to the Apostles; it was then distributed to any members who might be in need."

What follows in Acts are the contrasting stories of Joseph Barnabas and Ananias/Sapphira. The former sold a piece of land he owned and gave the proceeds to the Apostles. The latter, husband and wife, did the same but she convinced her husband to hold out a little for themselves.

Peter was astounded at their action. You owned the land to begin with, and it was yours to do with as you pleased, he said to them. When you sold it, the money was yours, also. Then you come and pretend you gave it all to us, but instead you lied and cheated. What was the point? You didn't lie to me; you lied to God.

The fate of Ananias and Sapphira remains a powerful example to those hypocrites who talk about helping the poor while, in reality, keeping money for themselves.

The sin of that couple was not their failure to give 100 percent to the poor. It was their pretense of giving 100 percent while keeping back a portion for themselves.

How much to give remains a burning question for the affluent. Jesus told the rich young man to sell everything. But Lazarus would have been content with only the leftovers. Is there a middle ground?

9. *How much do I give:*

In his second letter to the Corinthians (8: 1–15), St. Paul encourages them to give as generously as they can to the work of the church and to the poor. He writes about the people of Macedonia who "gave not only as much as they could afford but far more and quite spontaneously. . . .

"This does not mean that to give relief to others you ought to make things difficult for yourselves: it is a question of balancing what happens to be your surplus now against their present need, and one day they may have something to spare that will supply your own need. That is how we strike a balance: as Scripture says, 'The man who gathered much had none too much, the man who gathered little did not go short.'"

In quoting Exodus, Paul set down what Christians have been urged to follow for centuries: take what you need (not what you want) and give the rest away so that others will have what they need. To help the poor, the affluent do not have to starve themselves or consign themselves to live in shacks. God seeks fewer people living that way, not more. The way to wind up with fewer is for the affluent to share what they have without ending up among the poor they seek to help.

10. *A final word on Scriptures:*

There are many passages in the Old and New Testaments which speak about affluence, giving, and treasure. Searching them out is a way for the affluent to shape their consciences on their duties in justice.

For example, in Luke 6: 38, just after he has said "judge not," Jesus tells his listeners, "Give and there will be gifts for you: a full measure, pressed down, shaken together, and running over into your lap, because the amount you measure out is the amount you will be given back."

In that passage, Jesus vividly describes how giving wins rewards in return. But the return will not be more "things"; it will be treasures of a much more lasting nature.

Finally, also from Luke (12: 33–34), Jesus says this: "Sell your possessions and give alms. . . . For where your treasure is, there will your heart be also."

The question which each affluent person (that's you and me) must ask is this: Where is my heart? With God or money? With the Lazaruses of the world or the rich people?

From the Church

Just as the early church offered some elucidation on Jesus' words about money, giving, and justice, so the church throughout history has commented on affluence and its uses. Especially in recent decades, the popes have been commenting on the disparity between the wealthy and the poor. With the rise of industrialization, there came a rise in poverty. In an agrarian society, poverty was never as harsh. There were always berries to pick if nothing else. But with the cities came a new form of poverty, more desperate, less vincible. No berry trees grew in the mills of London and New York.

The industrial revolution also created great wealth for a few through wheeling and dealing (the polite term) or robber-baronry (less polite). The gap between the very rich and the very poor widened, and a new class of poverty was created: people who had jobs but were paid barely enough to survive. Child labor, endless working days, poor conditions, slums, ghettoes; these were some of the fruits of the mechanization of society.

In the face of this, popes in the last 100 years have been speaking again and again about the duties of the upper and middle classes toward the lower class and poor; of the employer toward the employees; of the employed toward the unemployed; of the industrialized toward the emerging; of the affluent toward the needy; of the free toward the oppressed.

These popes have seen, once more, the dangers which Jesus spoke of 2,000 years earlier: the dangers of materialism and wealth, of serving money instead of God, of selfishness and possessions.

What follows is a sampling of what they have observed:

1. *Rerum Novarum:*

Pope Leo XIII's 1891 encyclical, *Rerum Novarum* (On the Rights and Duties of Capital and Labor), is considered a pivotal document in the history of the church. This letter to the world addressed pressing issues of the times, including the relationship of capital and labor, the rights of workers, the purpose of unions, socialism, private property, the church and state, and wealth and poverty.

Responding to the rise of industrialism, Leo moved the church's teaching into the 20th century, shaping ancient thoughts to contemporary problems. One of those ancient thoughts is Jesus' words on the dangers of wealth.

"Those whom fortune favors are warned that riches do

not bring freedom from sorrow and are of no avail for eternal happiness," Leo wrote, "but rather are obstacles; that the rich should tremble at the threatenings of Jesus Christ—threatenings so unwonted in the mouth of our Lord—and that a most strict account must be given to the Supreme Judge for all we possess."

The Pope was referring specifically to the "alas" Beatitude, Jesus' warning that those who feast now will fast later.

How to evade the threat of Jesus? Leo continues: "It is one thing to have a right to the possession of money and another to have a right to use money as one wills. . . . How must one's possessions be used? The church replies without hesitation in the words of [Thomas Aquinas]: 'Man should not consider his material possessions as his own, but as common to all, so as to share them without hesitation when others are in need.'"

In short, the affluent cannot have what they want when others are *in* want. Need is the operative word. We have a right to what we need—and so do the poor.

In a paraphrase of Paul's words to the Corinthians, Leo notes, "True, no one is commanded to distribute to others that which is required for his own needs or those of his household; nor even to give away what is reasonably required to keep up becomingly his condition in life. . . . But, when what necessity demands has been supplied, and one's standing fairly taken thought for, it becomes a duty to give to the indigent out of what remains over."

The Pope goes on to stress that this duty is not required by human laws but by the "laws and judgments of Christ the true God, who in many ways urges on his followers the practice of almsgiving—'It is more blessed to give than to receive'; and who will count a kindness done or refused to the poor as done or refused to himself—'As long as you did it to one of my least brethren you did it to me.'"

Leo offers his own summary of his points:

"Whoever has received from the divine bounty a large share of temporal blessings, whether they be external and material, or gifts of the mind, has received them for the purpose of using them for the perfecting of his own nature, and, at the same time, that he may employ them, as the steward of God's providence, for the benefit of others."

To the affluent, Leo speaks clearly; their blessings are not for them to wallow in. Jesus, he stresses, has warned the rich (not only Onassis, Rockefeller, and Getty, but also us): not to share in this life means that, in the next, we will not share what the poor will be given.

What the affluent have been given is to be taken and used for two purposes: their own needs and the needs of others. The gifts of God are not given to be hoarded and stored in the contemporary barns of savings accounts, retirement plans, stock portfolios, and material possessions. Part of the blessings of God can be placed there for security and needs of the future, but part must also go to those in need.

2. *Quadragesimo Anno:*

Forty years after Leo's encyclical, Pope Pius XI issued a letter elucidating it. "On Reconstructing the Social Order" did not appear coincidentally on the anniversary of *Rerum Novarum;* it was planned as a sequel and expansion of Leo's thoughts on the issues of industrialization, socialism, materialism, and affluence.

As Leo did, Pius clearly states what must be done with "superfluous income, that is, income which (a person) does not need to sustain life fittingly and with dignity." Such income cannot be stuffed into our pockets or expended on ruby rings.

"Rather the Sacred Scriptures and the Fathers of the Church constantly declare in the most explicit language that the rich are bound by a very grave precept to practice almsgiving, beneficence, and munificence."

Again like Leo, Pius teaches that the disparity of blessings must be evened out by the affluent giving what they have in excess to those who have little. "To each," he writes, "must be given his own share of goods" in order to end "the huge disparity between the few exceedingly rich and the unnumbered propertyless." To do so, he states, is "social justice."

Are we the "exceedingly rich"? Or was he speaking to the Fords, Morgans, and Rockefellers of his time? If he was, do his words not apply to us? To a starving child of the Sahel, is a family in suburbia "exceedingly rich"? Is there a "huge disparity" between the average family of an RV camp and the average family of a refugee camp?

Is wealth evil, in Pius's view? Not wealth itself, but the misuse of it, a point he makes plainly:

"Those who are engaged in producing goods are not forbidden to increase their fortune in a just and lawful manner," he explains; "for it is only fair that he who renders service to the community and makes it richer should also, through the increased wealth of the community, be made richer himself according to his position, provided that all these things be sought with due respect of others and that they be employed in accordance with faith and right reason."

There is nothing wrong with wealth legitimately acquired. But there is something gravely wrong with the misuse of that wealth:

"The sordid love of wealth, which is the shame and great sin of our age, will be opposed in actual fact by the gentle yet effective law of Christian moderation which commands man to seek first the kingdom of God and his justice."

If people are moderate, Pius says, quoting the Bible, "temporal goods, insofar as (a person) has need of them, shall be given him." (Matthew 6: 33)

(Pius proceeds to make a distinction between justice and charity, a distinction which is interesting to note in passing. Affirming that justice means giving to each person "what is due him" or her, Pius nevertheless adds that "justice alone . . . can never bring about union of minds and hearts." Justice can end social conflict by leveling the gulfs between classes, he says, but charity will still be necessary to bring love, caring, and concern.)

3. *The Second Vatican Council:*

In 1965, the bishops of the world, meeting together with Pope Paul VI, issued a lengthy document on "The Church Today." Formally titled "Pastoral Constitution on the Church in the Modern World," the document is also known as *Gaudium et Spes* (Joy and Hope) from its opening words:

"The joys and the hopes, the griefs and the anxieties of

the men of this age, especially those who are poor or in any way afflicted, these too are the joys and hopes, the griefs and anxieties of the followers of Christ."

In that opening sentence, the Council restated a central teaching of the church from Christ's time: the problems of the world (including the poor) are the problems of all Christians and they must be addressed.

Chapter III of *Gaudium et Spes* is entitled "Socio-Economic Life." Like the other chapters (on such topics as the family, political life, and international relations), this one takes the changes in contemporary society and applies church teaching to them, shedding spiritual light on dark problems and offering solutions.

Many portions of the third chapter deal with affluence and poverty, and the widening gap between the two:

"While an enormous mass of people still lack the absolute necessities of life, some . . . live sumptuously or squander wealth. Luxury and misery rub shoulders. While the few enjoy very great freedom of choice, the many are deprived of almost all possibility of acting on their own initiative and responsibility, and often subsist in living and working conditions unworthy of human beings."

This contrast, the Council declared, can threaten "the very peace of the world" if it is not remedied through "justice and equity."

As both Leo and Pius did, the Council makes clear that it is legitimate for people to use money to make their own lives comfortable (recall the two popes' expressions: people can live "becomingly, fittingly, and with dignity"). In the words of *Gaudium et Spes,* people can spend their money "to cultivate (their) own material, social, cultural, and spiritual life worthily, and that of (their) dependents."

Beyond that, however, the affluent have a duty toward the needy because everyone has "the right to have a share of earthly goods sufficient for oneself and one's family. . . . Men are obligated to come to the relief of the poor and to do so not merely out of their superfluous goods."

What follows is a startling sentence:

"If a person is in extreme necessity, he has the right to take from the riches of others what he himself needs."

Remember the grade school question posed by every child after studying the seventh commandment: "Can I steal a loaf of bread if I am hungry?" The answer then was yes, but it didn't seem to matter since we had enough Wonder Bread to build a skyscraper even with the crust cut off. But the same principle, when applied to us today, has a disturbing sound: the poor have a right to take what they need from those who are affluent. "Extreme necessity" is the key phrase in the Council's sentence, but what is extreme necessity? Starvation? It exists, as the bishops went on to state:

"Since there are so many people in this world afflicted with hunger, this sacred Council urges all, both individuals and governments, to remember the saying of the Fathers: 'Feed the man dying of hunger, because if you have not fed him you have killed him.' According to their ability, let all individuals and governments undertake a genuine sharing of their goods."

(In a footnote, the Council quotes Pope John XXIII on the duty of the affluent toward the poor: "The obligation of every man, the urgent obligation of the Christian man, is to reckon what is superfluous by the measure of the needs of others, and to see to it that the . . . distribution of created goods serve(s) the common good.")

The Council (and Pope John) are in no way vague about the teaching: the affluent have a duty and obligation toward the poor; the poor can take what they need from the affluent; and the affluent must determine what they owe to the poor not by whimsy but by comparing what they have with what the needy have not.

"If you have not fed him, you have killed him." "What you do to the least of my brethren, you do to me." The juxtaposition of those two quotations is compelling.

4. *Pope John Paul II:*

In statement after statement, John Paul II has continued the tradition of Leo, Pius, and the Council by pointing out the dangers of materialism, the distress of the poor, and the obligations of the affluent.

In a homily on the Beatitudes, for example, John Paul emphasized that they cannot be picked apart like a bowl of fruit from which people select what they enjoy while passing over that which is distasteful.

"The Beatitudes are placed in antithesis to several values which are honored in the world," the Pope said in an obvious reference to the words of Jesus on poverty and wealth. "They stand and fall together. You cannot extract one of them and cultivate it at the expense of the others. It is not easy to be or want to be poor, meek, pure; nor to be persecuted, even for the sake of justice. But the kingdom of heaven is for nonconformists."

To conform to this world, he said another time, is "to be gorged with objects and gadgets." On yet another occasion, John Paul elaborated on the dangers of materialism:

"The consumer society—that excess of goods not needed by man—can, in a way, constitute an abuse of freedom when the more and more insatiable pursuit of goods is not subjected to the law of justice and of social love."

Justice is a constant refrain in the Pope's remarks on the state of the modern world. In his many tours of the globe, he again and again returns to a central theme of justice toward the needy and the remedy of the ills of consumerism, materialism, and greed.

In two encyclicals (*Redemptor Hominis* and *Dives in Misericordia*), John Paul starkly presents the contrast between affluence and poverty:

"We have before us a great drama that can leave nobody indifferent. The person who, on the one hand, is trying to draw the maximum profit and, on the other hand, is paying the price in damage and injury is always man. The drama is made still worse by the presence close at hand of the privileged social classes and of the rich countries, which accumulate goods to an excessive degree and the misuse of whose riches very often becomes the cause of various ills." (*Redemptor Hominis,* Redeemer of Man)

The "materialistic society . . . accepts the primacy of things over persons. . . . Side by side with wealthy and surfeited people and societies, living in plenty and ruled by consumerism and pleasure, the same human family contains individuals and groups that are suffering from hunger. There are babies dying of hunger under their mother's eyes. . . . [This] is increasing. It still happens that side by side with those who are wealthy and living in plenty there exist those who are living in want, suffering misery and often actually dying of hunger; and their number reaches tens, even hundreds of millions." (*Dives in Misericordia,* Rich in Mercy)

In the former encyclical, John Paul describes the state of things as representing "the gigantic development of the parable in the Bible of the rich banqueter and the poor man Lazarus."

The circle is closed. From Jesus' use of that parable 2,000 years ago to John Paul's allusion to it in our times, the story of the rich man and Lazarus haunts the world of the affluent and poor. Jesus, the church throughout history, papal documents in our time, and the Second Vatican Council have all warned against loving possessions more than people or God. Our love should not be directed at things. Rather, it should extend from our hearts to "all men and women without any exception or division; without difference of race, culture, language, or world outlook; without distinction between friends and enemies. This is love for people—it desires every true good for each individual and for every human community, every family, every nation, every social group, for young people, adults, parents, the elderly—a love for everyone, without exception. This is love . . . to ensure for each individual every true good, and to remove and drive away every sort of evil." (John Paul II, *Dives in Misericordia*)

Such love should drive away hunger and want, misery and cold, ignorance and disease. It is the affluent who can drive these away from the poor by examining themselves for what they have, what they need and what they want, and by contrasting those with what the poor have, need, and deserve.

4
Checking Our Checkbook

The task for each person is clear: to examine how affluent he or she is, and to compare that level of affluence with the condition of the poor. Side by side, shoulder to shoulder (to quote from the popes), we live with the poor, but each of us lives in uniquely different situations. We are an affluent people, but each of us stands on the scale at a different point. Some of us live in the castle down the highway; most of us live in the upper three floors; many of us are close to the cellar door.

There are ways to find out how we rate on the scale. We cannot determine our level of affluence simply by taking a guess or dreaming up a feeling. Guesses and feelings tend to be very self-aggrandizing. We feel pleased by our efforts toward the poor; we feel that our woes are the most distressing in the world; we feel pressed down by inflation; we feel we cannot do more than we are doing now.

Is that true? Perhaps it is. But to discover if it is, we have to examine ourselves more thoroughly. Here are some ways of doing that:

1. *The catalog test:*

Take the nearest merchandise catalog you can find. You might have a mail-order catalog lying around or perhaps you can find a circular that came with the daily newspaper.

Begin paging through. How many of the items shown inside do you want? How many do you have? How many do you need? How many do you have a right to? How many do the poor have a right to? How many should you possess while there are "mothers watching their children die of hunger"?

In any catalog, you might find such items as these:

- A $2,000 diamond pendant
- A pair of $200 ruby earrings
- A $10 key ring
- A $100 watch
- A $12 salt-and-pepper shaker set
- A $30 silverware set for eight
- A $10 copy of the Lord's prayer
- A $37 collector doll
- A $22 pipe set
- A $25 lighter
- A $287 electronic talking chess set
- A $20 wallet
- A $60 anniversary clock
- A $14 barometer
- A $17 ice bucket
- A $500 microwave oven
- A $19 hair dryer
- A $37 electric shaver
- A $70 rocking chair
- A $44 table lamp
- A $30 folding table
- A $275 camera
- A $104 radio
- A $250 stereo
- A $400 TV
- A $50 telephone
- A $230 calculator

- A $30 drill press
- A $100 chain saw
- A pair of $50 binoculars
- A $14 putter
- A $55 tennis racket
- A $30 camp stove
- A $100 shotgun
- A $120 bike
- A $25 toy organ

How many of these have you been thinking of buying? How many do you own? How many do you want (even if you can't afford them right now)? How many of them are necessities? How many of them are examples of what John Paul II called "objects and gadgets" that we "gorge" ourselves on? How many of them should be purchased, given the poverty in the world? If you had enough to buy one of them, what would convince you to take the money and give it instead to the poor?

It is a measure of our affluence that we have such catalogs in the first place. It is another measure that we turn to them to find something to buy. It is another that we don't think twice about making the purchase.

As the popes and the Council pointed out, we have a right to make our lives becoming, fitting, and dignified. We have a right to pursue cultural, material, social, and spiritual growth—worthily. Do the things we buy do this? Or are they merely signs of consumption, billboards of our affluence, ways of keeping up, methods of outdoing others, expressions of pride?

How affluent are you? The answers to the questions here will add up to the answer to that one question.

2. *The checkbook test:*

The record of our civilization is not contained in hieroglyphics on the side of a pyramid or in scrolls hidden in caves. It is written on the lines of our checkbooks. Stored on those scrawled notations are the ups and downs of our economy, the flow of our lives. From a checkbook, we can detect how our lives are going. Checks to the doctor and drug store indicate an illness. Checks to the liquor store and card shop indicate a party coming. The names of stores and credit card companies say that the first of the month has rolled around.

Take your checkbook for last year or even last month, and see where your money is going.

Here is a typical breakdown of the regular expenditures, through checks, of a family:

- Food
- Fuel, energy, gasoline
- Utilities
- Department stores, credit cards, loans
- Housing
- Insurance
- Medicine, doctors, dentists

To a large extent, the money spent on these is money spent to maintain life fittingly, becomingly, and with dignity. To a large extent, but not totally. Hidden in the food costs are dollars spent for Twinkies, cookies, brandy, sodapop, ice cream, and cole slaw. Mixed in the payments to department stores are dollars spent on luxuries and excess.

Then there are miscellaneous checks which give the

fingerprint of our individuality, checks made out to magazines, book clubs, ticket offices, newspapers, piano tuners, vets, hobby stores, health spas, travel agents, motels and hotels and restaurants, auto repair shops, and—you fill it in.

Finally, there are the checks to churches and charities.

Take a look at your year or month. What was the balance of these items? What "things" are represented by the check notations? Which were needed and which were wanted? How many could have been resisted? Did as much go to charity as to magazines and hobbies? Should it be the same, more, less?

How affluent are you? The answers to these questions will give you the answer to that one.

3. *The IRS test:*

Those who don't want to go back through their checkbooks can find, in their income tax forms, a handy compilation of how they have spent their income.

Listed there and totaled are income and outgo, where the money came from and where it went, how much went to mortgage and how much to charity.

Just take two lines: the one with your total income and the one with your total deductions for charity. How do they stand up next to each other? Under the biblical practice of tithing, which is gaining more and more prominence, 10 percent of income should be given to the needy. What percent of your income went to the poor, handicapped, forgotten, and less fortunate?

How affluent are you? The income line provides an answer and the charitable deductions line provides a way of comparing your blessings with those of others.

From Paul to John Paul, no one has asked the affluent to make themselves suffer for the poor. They have asked only that the affluent give of their extras so that those with nothing can have enough.

It is up to each person to decide what is enough. What is a luxury to one person might be a necessity to another. A microwave in one family might be a luxury; in a family with a single parent or two working parents, it might be a necessity. Material things (mixers, blenders, vacuum cleaners, dishwashers) rapidly move from being luxuries to being conveniences to being necessities. Whether that move is made in your individual home is for you to decide. The unique structure of your life, family, home, demands, interests, and other factors will determine at what point your enough becomes too much and at what point your too much becomes someone else's not enough.

Finding those points is not the work of an instant decision or vague feeling. It results from careful consideration and planning, from meditation on the words of Scripture and the church, from prayer, and from family discussion.

Once the points are found, we can proceed to the next step: determining how we will share our blessings, with whom, and how much.

5
Managing Our Money

We cannot give justice to others until we have given it to ourselves and our families. We cannot remedy the woes of others until we have solved our own imbalances. We have to get our own houses in order before we can offer to build one for someone else.

The right use of money includes using it properly for our own needs. Only when we have done that can we turn to aid others. We have a responsibility to look to our own requirements and to maintain the affluences we have, such as freedom, health, opportunity, and security. We also have the duty to pass them on to our children. Once we have done these things, we can make sure that others have their needs met.

It is, in the end, a balancing act. We walk a tightrope strung between our own needs and the needs of others. To stand on either end is to neglect the other side; the place to be is poised in the middle so that a delicate balance is struck. And that is not easy.

In times of economic unrest, no one is ever quite sure where the balance point is. It shifts almost daily. It's as though someone were shaking the tightrope as we traverse it, trying to topple us.

It is estimated, for example, that the average person works from January 1 to sometime in May just for the government. City, county, state, and federal taxes total so much that a worker might as well hand over his or her entire paycheck for the first four months-plus of every year just to get even.

Meanwhile, inflation continues. For every step forward in pay, workers take a step backward, thanks to inflation which turns increases into decreases. The paycheck is thus ravaged by both taxation and inflation. Consider, just to put it concretely, what inflation did to some products in the span from 1967 to 1981:

- 500 kilowatt hours of electricity jumped from $11 to $26
- A daily newspaper went from 10 cents to a quarter
- Steak soared from 69 cents a pound to $3
- A dozen eggs doubled in price
- A can of soup quadrupled in price
- Heating oil exploded from 17 cents a gallon to $1.20
- Phone service costs doubled
- A gallon of milk doubled in price and then some
- A pack of gum quintupled
- Sugar more than matched gum
- A movie ticket doubled

While some items stayed the same or dropped (TVs, electronic calculators), most took giant steps forward, making the purchase of a car or home prohibitive for many or financially draining for most.

In that same period, as taxes and inflation rose, families watched their children growing, with stomach capacity getting larger, tastes becoming more refined, clothing needed, and tuition costs arriving.

In the face of all this, people have found themselves strapped. Yet, as has been stated again and again, we are affluent. No one has found his or her family sleeping in the gutter. They may have put off buying a larger house or a second car; the vacation to Bermuda may have been postponed; the color TV might have been repaired instead of replaced—but the pressures on the family wallet did not cause massive starvation.

Families found ways to cope. When the kids needed clothes, discount houses were discovered. When tuition was needed, the summer job was invented. When energy costs soared, down went the thermostats.

There are plenty of attractive housing developments in America in which live affluent families. They may be sitting on hand-me-down furniture and eating pasta, but they are housed and fed. There may be orange crates behind the raised ranch's curtains, but no one is going hungry.

Comparatively speaking, we know that we are still affluent. The question remains: how do we handle our affluence justly, both for ourselves and for the needy?

Material Affluence

However much the paycheck is eaten into by taxation and inflation, it is still a paycheck and can be used in many different ways so that money is managed wisely and justly.

1. *Budgeting:*

Many people, who make the most detailed plans for a trip to the seashore, do nothing about their income. They make no budgets, plan no savings, outline no goals.

Most major expenses can be budgeted for. Housing,

food, loans on cars or tuition, insurance: these can be planned for. Christmas club savings accounts can be used to soften the blow of buying not only holiday gifts but also a major purchase down the road.

Setting and sticking to a budget helps families manage their money wisely, allowing them to have enough for important things and to save for the future.

2. *Saving:*

The proverbial rainy day comes to all people and saving for it is always necessary. Not all expenses can be foreseen. The roof leaks, the car breaks down, a medical need arises not covered by insurance: in cases such as these, savings are saviors.

One economist recommends that every family have six months' salary saved, providing a cushion for unemployment as well as unplanned problems and emergencies. Such an amount may be impractical for many families, but it gives a figure to aim for.

3. *Insurance:*

Like the hose behind the glass door, insurance is an "in case of" necessity. The newspapers are filled with articles of tragedy that strike an uninsured family. A house burns down and there is nowhere to go; a medical crisis occurs and there is no way to pay for the cure; a car is destroyed in an accident and there is no means of transportation; a breadwinner dies and there is nothing left behind.

Insuring life, house, and autos is a necessity in an affluent society. The loss of any of these (or the possibility of a suit from a car accident) requires the prudent use of insurance.

Insurance protects both the family and others, providing a cushion in times of trouble. Health insurance is also a necessity, given the rising costs of medical care.

No matter the kind of insurance, shopping for it is the wise way to proceed. Don't stick with one company; look around. Don't go for the first offer. Don't buy the maximum on the assumption that you need a millionaire's protection.

4. *Shopping around:*

With inflation, more and more people are learning to bargain hunt, to shop around, to wait for sales, to comparison shop. To walk in a store and buy the first item seen is an improper use of money; it abdicates the responsibility to spend each penny intelligently.

A woman I know never settles for the list price. Even after she has compared from store to store, she goes into negotiation with the owner, bargaining for additional features or free delivery or a further reduction. Shopping for a washer and dryer, for example, she began by finding a combination that cost $1,000 in a prestigious store. From there, she went to discount centers, checking out the same or comparable models. When she found the cheapest list price, she began haggling. When she was done, she ended up paying less than $600 for better models, got free delivery and a few extras. Plus she kept her old appliances. She gave away her dryer to a friend and sold the washer to a scrap dealer.

5. *Loans and time-payments:*

As inflation has risen into the stratosphere, it has lifted with it interest rates and charges for borrowing money (either directly or in the form of purchases when a credit card is used).

Credit card charges border on the usurious, but they are hidden by being added surreptitiously every month. Consumers who use credit cards indiscriminately are misusing their money because they are spending dollars they don't have and will end up paying far more for something than originally charged.

The temptation of plastic money is almost diabolic. It doesn't seem to cost anything when you sign your name on a thin sheet of paper and walk away with a glittering prize. But the cost comes, once a month, sometimes forever.

Avoiding credit card buying is a wise effort. Many people have taken to cutting up their cards to end the temptation for good.

As for borrowing money, it is seldom a wise idea. Taking a loan in order to fly to Florida is a luxury few should defend. Borrowing it to do other things—buy a car, for example, or make home repairs—is more defensible but leaves the person with an albatross to carry for years.

6. *Doing without:*

Saying no to the urge to buy is not easy for most Americans. It is so easy to say yes. There are advertisements to lure us in, packaging to make us pick it up, salespeople to affirm our desires, and credit cards to make it painless.

But the piper has to be paid the first of every month. Doing without is better in many cases. Trips to Disney World can become weekends at the nearby amusement park. The second car can become the public transportation system. A new couch can be a recovered old one.

People considering a purchase should go back and ask the basic question: Do we really need this?

7. *Doing with less:*

The answer to that question might be yes, but another one remains: Do we really need this particular model or version or style?

Doing with less—turning down thermostats, leaving the car in the garage while walking to the store, buying a stripped-down model, purchasing fewer—is a way of filling needs while also saving.

8. *Investing:*

The wise use of money includes the wise management of it as well as the wise expenditure of it. Various methods of investing money exist, each providing some unique advantage. There are money market certificates and six-month savings accounts for high interest; there are stocks and municipal bonds for speculation; there are individual retirement programs for future planning; there are bank insurance offers; there are investments in gold and silver.

Taking left-over income and sticking it in a regular savings account has become, for many Americans, the least they can do to make their money work for them. Establishing a sound, secure, and advantageous system of investment requires thought, planning, consultation, intelligence, and some risk. It cannot be done haphazardly or on the advice of someone's brother-in-law who made a killing in corn futures.

9. *Old age and death:*

These are two topics the young couple with a newborn never wants to think about, but planning for the future is necessary for a sound use of money. Everyone should have a will and preplanned funeral arrangements. After a home, a funeral (not a car) is a person's most expensive single purchase. To leave that purchase to a distraught survivor is to handle money foolishly. And to die intestate is to leave your money to lawyers, the government, and the whim of Byzantine laws.

Planning early for retirement is also wise. Joining a pension program at work or establishing an individual retirement program through a bank supplements Social Security, a supplement more and more elderly people are finding to be lifesaving.

As the longevity of Americans is increased, the necessity of planning for the years after age 65 becomes plainer. Such planning removes a future financial burden from your children and the government, while also providing you with a means of maintaining independence.

Here's a checklist for seeing how you have handled your material affluence:

( ) I have a budget for housing, food, medical costs, insurance, and loans.

( ) I stick to those budgets 10 out of every 12 months.

( ) I have a savings program that sets aside a certain amount from every paycheck.

( ) That savings program is supplemented by a diversified investment program.

( ) I have adequate but not extravagant insurance on my house, car, life, and health.

( ) I shop around and bargain hunt. When the kids need clothes, I don't buy them designer jeans. When they need shoes, I don't buy them the "in" sneaker. When I make a major purchase, I compare prices.

( ) I avoid using my credit cards whenever I can. If I don't have the money to buy something, I do without.

( ) Doing without and doing with less have become my bywords. In the last year, I have turned the thermostat down ______ degrees, driven my car ______ fewer miles, resisted buying ______ and ______.

( ) I have made a will.

( ) I have made my funeral arrangements.

( ) I have an adequate retirement program.

( ) In general and as a rule, I buy what I need, not what I want.

For most people, material affluence results from employment. Few of us subsist on inheritance or the income from investments. We work for our bucks and try to make our bucks work a little for us. Our lives revolve around our jobs. We try to balance them with our families and keep our perspective. We try to spend as much time with our children as with our boss, to be at home as much as we are at work, to think about our families as much as we think about our work, to put as much into raising our children as into raising our salaries.

So the right use of money includes an examination of the source of our money. We cannot justify doing anything for cash. That's obvious when we think of the extremes. We would not murder for money and we hold prostitutes in low regard. "Anything for a buck" is an expression we use pejoratively.

But have we examined our work with the eyes of justice? What do we do for our dollars? Here's a list of questions to ask yourself, think about, and discuss as a family (where appropriate):

- What do I do for a living?
- What does it produce for others? How does it benefit people?
- How do I perform my job? Conscientiously? With skill, enthusiasm, intelligence?

- Am I fairly paid? Do I deserve more?
- Am I using all my talents in my work and giving fully of my time to my employer?
- Do I help others with their work by doing mine properly, on time, in cooperation with them?
- Am I keeping someone else from advancing by blocking their efforts?
- How secure is my job? How secure should it be? Can it be? Have I made it secure by doing a good job or by becoming irreplaceable?
- Am I ethical in my dealings with customers, employers, fellow workers?
- Should I seek other work in another line or another business because I am wasted where I am now or not doing an adequate job?
- What does my employer owe me? What do I owe him?

If you are an employer, foreman, shop steward, head cashier, or otherwise in charge of other workers, there are more questions:

- How do I treat those under me?
- Am I fair in my dealings with others?
- Do I deserve respect? Do I give it?
- Do those under my control do their best? Can I correct them?
- How would those under me work if they followed my example—better or worse?
- Do I produce safe, usable, needed goods and products and services?

A job is not a license to steal, to ignore the needs of

others, to step on people, to behave ruthlessly, or to oppress. A job is a source of material affluence and must be approached with a constant eye for morality, justice, and ethics. Our gifts and talents play a role in our ability to work; it is a blessing to be able to perform a service, carry out a function, offer a skill or do something for which others will pay you. That blessing is not given to all in equal measure—another reason why those who are blessed in that way must pay attention to the demands of justice. The fruits of our labor must be shared with all.

As Paul and the popes and the Vatican Council pointed out, we have a right to use those fruits to benefit ourselves and our families first. In the words of the Council, "Payment for labor must be such as to furnish a man with the means to cultivate his own material, social, cultural, and spiritual life worthily and that of his dependents."

Money from employment, therefore, can rightly be spent on yourself and family for a number of purposes. Break down the list given by the Council and consider the ways in which each of us can justly spend income:

Material life: food, clothing, housing, toys, furniture, savings.

Social life: trips to visit friends and family, vacations, dinners with family and friends, parties.

Cultural life: books, magazines, TVs, radios, stereos, tape recorders, tours of other countries, tickets to plays and movies and concerts.

Spiritual life: pilgrimages, subscriptions to religious periodicals, spiritual books and tapes.

A wide range of items can be purchased for legitimate use by a family as long as they are "worthy" (or, to use other synonyms, fitting, becoming, dignified). What's worthy and what isn't? Of course, that's for each person to decide after thought and prayer. But here's a suggested list of how some items might break down:

- Clothing: a pair of pants is worthy; designer jeans are not.
- Food: roast beef is worthy; caviar is not.
- Housing: a three-bedroom home is worthy; a mansion is not.
- Toys: a truck is worthy; a motorized rocking horse is not.
- Furniture: a chair is worthy; an antique you can't sit on anyway is not.
- TV: a 19-inch color set is worthy; a large-screen projection system with stereo sound is not.
- Magazines: a subscription to *Time* is worthy; a year's supply of *Penthouse* is not.
- Pilgrimage: a visit to Lourdes is worthy; a sabbatical on Waikiki is not.

Agree or disagree? It doesn't matter. What matters is that each person consider his or her own circumstances and draw some lines, dividing worthy life from sheer luxury, separating living with dignity from basking in wealth. To live on one side of those lines is to live justly, using affluence rightly. To live on the other side is to cheat the poor and to reject justice.

Intangible Affluence

The other affluences of our lives—freedom, health, opportunity, security, and hope—must be handled in the same way we handle material affluence. We must check ourselves to see how we use them in our own lives before we can determine how to share them with others. Are we meeting the needs of ourselves and our families in these affluences?

1. *Freedom:*

Preserving and defending freedom, without tumbling into jingoism or chauvinism, is not easy. It is always tempting to turn patriotism into an overpowering pride which says me-first and us-only and let-the-rest-go-to-the-devil.

But freedom is an affluence we must hold on to and maintain, keeping the extremes away. To love freedom does not mean to bomb others or to scorn another nation or to overthrow another government. It means behaving freely but not licentiously. It means taking on the duties of freedom (voting intelligently, participating in government, seeking the redress of grievances) as well as defending the rights of others to do the same.

Preserving freedom also requires us to pass it on to our children, to give them a sense of what freedom is and how precious liberty is. It means teaching them the difference between love of country and hatred of others, between freedom and license, between law and anarchy, between love of flag and a slavish devotion to it that borders on idolatry.

To do these things may mean the expenditure of money: to join organizations, to buy books and magazines, to visit Washington, D.C., to write congressional or state representatives. This is a proper use of income, for it turns money into the preservation of a worthier affluence.

2. *Health:*

This affluence can become the most neglected one. It's

easy, when feeling good, to forget about maintaining health, but it is a duty to do so.

That means eating right, exercising, having regular check-ups, practicing preventive medicine, using pills properly—and teaching children to do the same.

Keeping healthy can be expensive. It costs money to have health insurance and dental coverage, to buy nutritious food rather than junk, to visit the doctor or dentist when you don't have to, to send your kids to eye doctors when they see fine, to join an exercise club. But it is money well spent.

At one time or another, everyone has known the debilitation of being ill. Being sick, for even a short period, soon enervates and eventually destroys. To invite illness by ignoring health is a misuse of the blessing of soundness.

3. *Opportunity:*

Maintaining the affluence of opportunity means making use of it. We must avoid stagnation—in our jobs and lifestyles, in our beliefs and talents. We must constantly challenge and question ourselves. Perhaps we will come back to our original starting point, perhaps we will change and grow, but, either way, we will be different for having used the affluence of opportunity.

We have the opportunity to educate ourselves, to travel, to listen to other views, to change jobs, to do any number of things which will mature us, deepen our knowledge, or make us better people.

The Vatican Council called it developing ourselves culturally and socially. Unlike many people in the world (who have been thwarted politically or by their lack of material affluence), we have the opportunity to do these things.

We also have the responsibility of telling our children about their opportunities. We have to free them from our expectations and dreams to let them have their own. We have to remind them constantly that they are special individuals with their own choices to make. We have to open the door to the world for them and let them out on their own.

4. *Security:*

To make use of the affluence of security, we have to work hard. It involves political action in crime control, prison reform, police review, neighborhood unity, and law changes. It means protecting yourself and your family with prudence and not paranoia. It also means developing a sense of secureness within the home.

5. *Hope:*

All of the previous affluences add up to this one. Because of the others, we have hope. We may face problems, but we have the freedom to fight them, the opportunity to change them from problems into pluses. For all the tribulations of life (and they are many), we remain hopeful because we have ways to confront troubles, to stand off woes, to deal with grief, to handle disappointment, to wipe away tears.

Instilling this sense of hope in ourselves and our children is not really difficult. It comes with the knowledge that we are affluent.

6
Some Practical Suggestions

Suppose you were handed $200,000. What would you do with it?

Give it some thought. What would you do with a windfall of that proportion?

In 1979, Mother Teresa of Calcutta received approximately that much when she won the Nobel Peace Prize. She turned the entire amount over to the poor, building homes, buying food, stocking medical centers.

In 1980, Adolfo Perez Esquivel won $212,000 when he took the Peace Prize. He donated the money to programs—education, publications, training—to improve the lot of the oppressed majorities of the world.

Every now and then, the newspapers headline the teenage girl, the elderly couple, or the just plain Joe and Jane who won a lottery. Invariably, the person pledges some of the winnings to the needy. A teenage girl in Ohio, for example, promised part of her winnings to help educate her brothers and sisters, and part to be donated to underprivileged children.

What would you do with the money?

What do you do with the money you have?

Once we have settled our own finances and seen to the right use of our income to supply us with what we need, there is some left over. Why? Because we are affluent. What is left-over can go for luxuries and treats, extras and gifts. But it should not. Justice demands that it be given to the less affluent.

Taking from our surplus (and even from our own money) and giving it to the poor is not an act of charity. It is a demand of justice, for all the reasons we have already examined. It is also a demand of justice to see to the efficient distribution of our gift. It is wrong to withhold our blessings from the unblessed; it is also wrong to give it haphazardly, ineffectively, or foolishly.

The usual outlet for our sharing with the poor is charity. (But, to emphasize the point again, we must remember that this giving is not charity; it is justice. It is the right of the poor to have a good life; it is our duty to help them have it.) Selecting a charity from among the thousands at work takes some time and thought, efforts necessary to assure that our giving is used as fully as possible.

Appeals come in the mails all the time. We call it "junk mail" and often toss it out without opening it. We get requests to feed the hungry, educate the ignorant, cure the sick, clothe the naked, soothe the distraught, house the homeless. We are begged to give relief to those caught in some natural disaster, to help the Indians of India and the Indians of the plains, to support the downtrodden, and to welcome refugees.

Then there are the pleas to use our material affluence to foster the intangible affluences of the world: to protect disappearing species, to clean the air, to ban handguns, to eliminate racism, to promote women's rights, to guard the Constitution, to back one political party or another, to safeguard this amendment or that.

Each of us will respond to these in different ways, giving to some of the causes, rejecting others randomly, casting some off because we don't agree with the position itself or the methods used in promoting it. But our response should be reasoned and ordered. Our giving to the needy—our being just—should be done with some rationality behind it.

Here are some ways of doing so:

1. *Picking charities:*

The occasional scandal within a charitable organization, revealing that only ten cents of every dollar given gets to the needy or that the upper echelon is skimming money from the pot, reminds us, with a shock, that not all charities are idealistic groups dedicated to carrying on the work of Jesus.

There are, to be blunt, crooks out there.

Avoiding them takes some careful footwork, a two-step called the "don'ts" and "do's":

Don't automatically give to everyone who puts his or her hand out while wearing an expression of soulful need. We are approached through the mails and in malls, in shopping center parking lots and on our doorsteps, via telethons and telephone calls. The natural instinct is to give, either to be kind or to get rid of the beggar. That instinct should be abandoned.

Do offer, when approached, to take informational brochures and to look into the cause. This gives you a chance to examine the organization in greater detail and to determine who they are and if they deserve your money.

Do contact offices which can guide you in picking a charity. The first office might be of the charity itself. Request from it a copy of its latest financial statement, showing where donations go and how much is subtracted in administrative fees. If the charity won't come across, don't you either. Another office to check with: the city, county, or state government office in charge of registering charities. Better Business Bureaus, Chambers of Commerce, and other community groups also keep lists of responsible charities. If the charity is religiously affiliated, you can check with the nearest central office of that denomination to find out if they are truly soliciting funds.

Don't be afraid to say no if you have doubts about someone asking for a donation.

2. *Planning your giving:*

Getting some general idea of which charities and causes are legitimate and responsible is one step. The next is to select the specific ones to whom you are going to give your money.

How do you decide? Two people stand before you asking for money to help the needy. Into which hand do you place your check? Do you divide it?

The goal is to make your gift count. That can be done by giving all of your gifts to one group. It can also be accomplished by sharing with as many as you can, counting on others to supplement your money.

Each of us has some special interests, which arise from our background and personalities. A family with a handicapped member might feel especially called to give to medical charities. A person who has been raised in poverty might feel moved to concentrate on giving to the hungry. Someone touched deeply by a cause (abortion, capital punishment, nuclear disarmament) might turn in those directions.

It is likely that we feel pulled in several directions at once, which means making some difficult choices. We cannot dispense our money willy-nilly; to do so weakens its effectiveness and our own sense of fulfilling what we are required to do.

So we have some hard questions to answer:

Can I give to save the whales when human beings are starving?

Can I give to a hospital research center when there are hungry children? A child in braces cannot walk, but he or she can eat and sleep; a hungry child can walk but goes to bed with an empty feeling.

Can I donate money to a campaign to restore returnable bottles when thousands are homeless because of an earthquake?

Do baby seals deserve my money as much as baby humans?

Should I give to help women gain their equal rights or to help men and women gain a decent living?

The answers will be different for each individual. There are no right and wrong answers. The important thing is to give and to make that gift count as much as possible. There are many ways of responding to the demands of justice. The key is to respond.

3. *Here or there?*

"Afghanistanism" is a word in journalism circles. It refers to the practice of newspapers condemning something far away while ignoring a similar problem close at hand. It's easy to write editorials about the government of some nation halfway around the globe; it's more difficult to attack city hall.

Afghanistanism applies to giving, too. It's easy to fall prey to the idea that the needy live only in Calcutta or on Africa's deserts. In fact, they live downtown, across the block, around the corner.

It's important to remember that the needy need, no matter where they live. The hungry child who speaks English feels as bad as the hungry child who speaks Hindi. The house of brick is as needed as the house of mud.

In giving, we should not forget local charities, nationwide, statewide, and city-centered.

4. *Other gifts:*

Money is not our only material affluence and a check is not the only gift that is needed by the poor. There are other material needs which charities seek and which we can give.

Clothing drives are held regularly by groups seeking to provide decent clothes for the poor. Our affluent closets bulge with dresses a size too small, sportscoats long out of style, shoes we've cast aside, and jackets we replaced last Christmas.

Many charities such as the St. Vincent de Paul Society and the Salvation Army seek furniture. Counseling services for unwed mothers always need baby clothes, children's furniture, and other infant items. Some groups look for toys (used and new) to brighten the lives of poor kids. Educational centers for the marginally retarded and handicapped often seek small appliances and other items to help in their teaching programs.

5. *Other places:*

Many people are looking for donations to help with their work, even though that work is not immediately feeding the hungry or comforting those struck by tragedy.

On our list of charities, we can include peace coalitions, justice centers, counseling agencies, homes for battered wives and unwed mothers, and other groups which work not only on long-range relief but also on protecting or providing the intangible affluences. Through our material gift, we can help assure that intangible affluences—freedom, opportunity, security, health, and hope—will reach those less fortunate than we.

To give someone freedom, donate to a group which protects human rights (Amnesty International, for example, or Pax Christi).

To give someone health, give to a group which brings medical care to areas which are without doctors (such as Project Hope or the Red Cross).

To offer someone security, support those who shelter alcoholics, battered women, or parolees.

To bring someone hope, give to mission societies which offer religious education and spiritual presence.

To offer someone opportunity, back organizations which aid refugees or help minorities.

6. *Some suggestions:*

A complete list of charities would fill volumes; what follows are some suggestions of Catholic groups you might want to investigate. They offer a wide range of services to the needy:

• Catholic Relief Services (1011 First Ave., New York, NY 10022) provides overseas relief aid in emergency situations and long-range help to the needy, such as providing education in farming techniques and materials for getting started. CRS collects from Catholics at Masses one weekend a year, makes ad hoc appeals in dire situations (a drought in Africa, an earthquake in Latin America) and accepts donations anytime.

• Campaign for Human Development (1312 Massachusetts Ave., NW, Washington, D.C. 20005) provides assistance to the needy in America by supporting self-help projects and seeding programs to solve problems. CHD, which is also supported through an annual collection, funds such projects as legal aid assistance, agricultural improvement, housing rehabilitation, and food banks.

• Several Catholic organizations provide help to the hungry of the world through foster parent programs. The affluent here support a specific child, person, or family overseas, following their progress and keeping in touch personally. The Catholic Near East Welfare Association (1011 First Ave., New York, NY 10022) sponsors foster children in the Middle East. The Pontifical Institute for Foreign Missions operates a Foster Parents Mission Club (35750 Moravian Drive, Fraser, MI 48026) with children in such areas as India and Bangladesh.

• Societies for the Propagation of the Faith exist in every diocese in the nation, supporting medical, educational and spiritual efforts around the world.

• Organizations which help the needy minorities of America through missionary efforts also exist. The Catholic Negro-American Missions Board (335 Broadway, New York, NY 10013) and the Commission for Catholic Missions Among the Colored People and the Indians (2021 H St. NW, Washington, D.C. 20006) are two such groups.

• Pax Christi, USA (300 N. Mango Ave., Chicago, IL 60634) works, as part of the International Catholic Movement for Peace, on such issues as nuclear disarmament and human rights.

• There are numerous groups working in the area of medicine, health, and aid for the handicapped. There are organizations for the deaf, blind, and physically handicapped, for the mentally disabled, for overseas medical assistance, and for domestic health care. To find out about them, contact your local diocesan chancery, office of Catholic Charities, or Society for the Propagation of the Faith.

• There are also many groups working in other areas such as communication, spiritual renewal, and education. They include the Christophers (12 E. 48th St., New York, NY 10017), Worldwide Marriage Encounter (3711 Long Beach Blvd., Suite 204, Long Beach, CA 90807), and the parish school in your area.

• In your local area, there are also hospitals, homes for unwed mothers, shelters for the indigent, hostels for drug abusers, counseling centers for alcoholics and those facing marital difficulty, youth centers, homes for the aged, jail ministries, and many more places crying for aid.

You can help one of them or a lot of them. You can give to a single agency or give to an umbrella organization. Whatever your individual choice, it should be done intelligently, with an eye on the effectiveness of the group, its stewardship of the money that comes to it, and its standing in the community.

Giving in Other Ways

The donation of money is one (very important) way of fulfilling the duty of the affluent to help the needy so that justice is done. But there are other ways. We have other gifts. Material affluence, as we have noted again and again, is not our only blessing. We have a responsibility to share our other blessings: time, abilities, health, talents, skills.

Recall the words of Leo XIII: "Whoever has received from the divine bounty a large share of temporal blessings, whether they be external and material, or gifts of the mind, has received them for the purpose of using them . . . for the benefit of others. 'He that has a talent,' said St. Gregory the Great, 'let him see that he hide it not; he that has abundance, let him quicken himself to mercy and generosity; he that has art and skill, let him do his best to share the use and the utility hereof with his neighbor.' "

Here are some ways of donating nonmonetary blessings to the needy:

1. *Health:*

If you have a healthy body, you can share it with those afflicted with disease—a literal sharing. Giving blood is a simple procedure which saves lives. It costs the giver nothing; it saves the person facing surgery.

There is another way of sharing a healthy body: by donating parts of it, after death, to be given to others. After our death, our eyes, kidneys, and other organs can be used by others so they can see, live fully, and be kept safe from debilitation. Everyone should carry a card which gives permission for transplants to be made after death.

2. *Time:*

All of us have extra time which we expend uselessly by watching TV, napping, puttering in the garden, or otherwise "killing time." Recreation is a good thing; idleness is not. Rather than kill time, we should use it for others by volunteering to work for them—in hospitals, at church, for a neighbor. The work might be manual or intellectual, emotional or spiritual. It might mean pushing a wheelchair or listening to the person in it. It could mean wielding a paint brush in the parish hall or coaching Little League. It might be bringing communion to the housebound or working in the garden of the elderly person next door.

3. *Comfort:*

Two questions:

A. Is it justifiable to keep your thermostat at 70 degrees (68? 66? 64?) when there are people freezing to death? Could the money saved by lowering the temperature of your house be donated to someone who is homeless?

B. After planning your next vacation, could you subtract one day of it and give the money saved to those who are condemned to live their lives totally within the confines of a barrio? (Going away for five days? Go for four and give one-fifth of what you would have spent to the poor.)

4. *Opportunity:*

The affluent are free to seize whatever opportunities come their way. Is it always just to do so? Offered a moonlighting job, but not really needing the money, could you turn it down so that an unemployed person could take it?

If you are a person returning to the work force after raising a family but not really needing the income—could you let the opportunity pass into the hands of someone without a job? Could you find the same fulfillment of your skills in volunteer work?

5. *Talents and skills:*

Everyone has some special ability—to draw, to work with wood, to wallpaper rooms, to sculpt, to decorate, to arrange flowers, to sing. Everyone has something they do (besides their work) which is a hobby they have pursued and perfected.

That talent or skill can be given to the needy. Nursing homes need people to teach residents hobbies. Homes for the handicapped and hospitals seek people who can provide manual training. Programs are always looking for ways of cutting corners and saving on repairs. The bedridden need to be entertained and visited.

6. *Two easy ones:*

A. Retired people have talents and skills—and the time to give them to others.

B. Everyone can participate in consumer boycotts which seek to help the hungry, back workers, or redress grievances. Just because it's easy to do (not to eat X and to replace it for a while with Y) doesn't mean it's not effective.

7. *Freedom:*

Sacrificing freedom and privacy is not easy. It means giving up a part of ourselves. Writing a check is one thing; going to volunteer somewhere is a little more difficult; but bringing someone into our homes is perhaps the hardest of all.

Yet there are programs which seek homes for people: unwed mothers, battered wives, refugees, foreign students.

To bring a stranger in requires us to be open, generous, and loving.

"I was a stranger and you took me in," Jesus said when he asked us to see in the needy his face.

8. *Working with others:*

Not every effort we expend for the poor has to be done solo. There are organizations to join and many parishes have committees which serve the needy. Being a part of a community effort eases the burden of giving our time, skills, and selves.

Consider the case of St. Maurice parish, Fort Lauderdale, Florida. In one year, the parishioners there combined to give nearly $80,000 to the hungry all over the world.

"It's the number one responsibility people have as Christians," explains the pastor. To which a parishioner adds, "We have everything at St. Maurice. Why not help those who don't have anything? I couldn't understand why God was letting hunger happen. Then I realized it's us who are letting it happen. I had all these luxuries and there were people out there starving. The reality just hit me that the world is so lopsided and something had to be done."

So the people of the parish began eating simple meals once a month and donating the money that would have been spent on a more elaborate meal. Special activities were held to raise money, and a portion of the annual parish fair was set aside for the hungry. The parish now supports a mission and medical clinic in a Bogota slum, a nutrition center and nursery in Guatemala, a hot lunch program in Thailand, and three water projects in Central Africa. In addition, the parish sponsors five foster children and is looking soon to have 100 families each support a child. And while reaching out to the Cambodians, the parish also provides hot meals to the infirm elderly of their own city.

"It's the way we live that counts," said the pastor. "It's wrong to go overboard building rectories and churches while people are dying."

Explained a parishioner: "It's what God wants us to do. It's written all over the Bible. Feed the hungry. And he's talking to us now."

By pooling their resources and energies, their common faith and their affluence, the people of St. Maurice parish are touching people scattered around the globe, making neighbors of people on the Florida coast and people in refugee camps.

There are groups other than parishes which work to feed the hungry and bring justice to the world. There are organizations that fight injustice on the human rights level (Amnesty International), on the corporate level (the Interfaith Coalition for Corporate Responsibility), on ad hoc bases as well as on the level of supplying food, clothing, and other essentials of life.

9. *Even more ways:*

There are additional, nonmonetary ways to help those in need and to bring justice to the world. In a talk to a group of nuns, Immaculate Heart of Mary Sister Amata Miller said, "Make choices in solidarity with the poor. Be an advocate, lobby for an issue, write letters to the editor, participate in boycotts and educate. Use all the media available to teach Christian social principles. We are stewards, not absolute owners, of God's gifts to us."

Her words apply to everyone. Each of us can press for changes in government aid so that the poor benefit. That pressing can include informing legislators of our feelings, making them known through the media (letters to editors, calls to radio talk shows) and discussing them with our friends.

It is often forgotten that our tax money goes, to a large extent, to help the needy. When we think of the ways in which we help the poor and share our affluence, we should not forget taxes. The government (perhaps clumsily, sometimes inefficiently, occasionally corruptly) feeds the hungry through Food Stamps, educates children through public schools, cares for the sick through Medicaid and Medicare, supports the elderly through Social Security, and performs all sorts of good deeds through what is commonly (and all too often derisively) known as "welfare."

It is each citizen's duty to see to it that tax revenues are spent wisely, effectively, and with minimal bureaucracy. A great portion of our affluent income goes to the needy through taxation. We should not forget that or ignore it. It is a process we should be involved in.

We should also be involved in determining what percentage of our taxes goes to the poor and needy and what percentage goes to other programs. Setting the right balance is a work of justice.

"In the United States," Sister Amata pointed out, "seven times as much money is spent on alcoholic beverages as is given in foreign aid. The U.S. contains 5 percent of the world's population and consumes 25 percent of the goods and services."

Setting those balances right is the work of each of us

individually. Setting another balance right is the work of an informed and united citizenry:

"I often think how much the cost of a single bomber could contribute toward building schools, nutrition centers, and homes so children of the poor could lead a happier life," said Adolfo Perez Esquivel, the 1980 Nobel Peace Prize recipient.

The estimated cost of a bomber in the U.S. is $30 million. Annually the nations of the world expend half a trillion dollars on armaments. Against such massive figures, the millions spent on welfare programs turn out to be puny. If the balance were changed, wonders could be accomplished, in the view of James Grant, executive director of the United Nations Children's Emergency Fund (UNICEF):

Stop building two bombers a day, he estimates, and the world could end poverty by the year 2000. Divert $50 million a day from armaments and apply it to fighting hunger and the grim statistics of starvation could be reversed. Currently three out of every ten Third World children die before the age of five and not even one in ten is seen by a health worker or immunized against common diseases which no one should contract anymore.

10. *Prayer:*

"It is important to remind ourselves," said Perez Esquivel, "that we are brothers and sisters in Christ, and that those in need of liberation cry for support and solidarity, particularly the humble, the ones who suffer oppression and persecution.

"When I said help, I mean especially prayers, for I believe in the power of prayer."

A State of Mind

To help those in need, to bring justice where there is misery, to share our affluence with those less blessed, we have to develop, first of all, a proper frame of mind about the poor.

The poor are not "them." The poor are "us," because we are one in Christ. God is not a cosmic Santa Claus who stays in the department store labeled "America," dispensing goodies our way because we are particularly good little boys and girls. God is God to everyone and he sometimes calls upon us to be his helpers in bringing the gifts of life to the world.

One day I was driving along a freeway with my family, and we exited onto a street in the inner city. My son, then nine, looked around at the ramshackle buildings, the dirty streets, the clothes hanging on lines, and the dark faces.

"Is this a bad street?" he asked.

I had to think a moment. It isn't a bad street; it's a poor street. But, to too many people, poor equals bad. They give moral dimensions to poverty and see in poverty a sign of God's disfavor.

So we are tempted to look down on the poor, to see them as inferior, to treat them as sinners, to regard them as less human. We are tempted to label them "shiftless" or to demean them. We draw up stereotypes and comfort ourselves with the fictional images. People on welfare, so many of us believe, are healthy black men driving Cadillacs and living high off our tax money.

The reality of welfare recipients—that they are primarily white, most often single parents, frequently children, often handicapped in some way—is never allowed to intrude. We hear the stories of people pulling up in taxis to cash their welfare checks, and we latch onto the myths. The one cheat out of 1,000 becomes our model for all of "them"—because it is comforting to think of them that way; it relieves us of the duty to help them, to think about them, to consider their rights.

Before we are going to be just, we have to be fair. We have to give to poor people equal dignity with ourselves and an equal place in God's scheme. It is no disgrace to be poor; if it were, Jesus would be the most disgraceful man ever to have lived.

The first justice we owe the needy is not material or intangible, it is not our time or skills or checks. The first thing we owe them is respect. When we have given that, our other giving will come more easily for we will be giving to ourselves and to Jesus, who told us to see him in those we help.

Once we have given that respect and begin our delivery of justice to the people in the world's cellar, we will not be frustrated. We will avoid the temptation of demanding immediate and observable results of our giving. Our gift may be a drop in the bucket, but it is a drop which would be missing had we not given it. And we can be confident that others will be adding their gifts as well.

We cannot expect to change the world or save it by our efforts alone. We must be content that we have helped it to some immeasurable but real degree.

If we give to a foster child overseas, comfort an ill person in the hospital nearby, write a letter to a congressman about taxes—if we do anything to help bring justice, we can't expect morning headlines declaring an end to hunger or a millenium of peace. But we cannot be discouraged either. What we do for others helps them and us; that should be enough.

How Cheap Are You?

It is natural, when assessing ourselves in any way, to give ourselves a break. Sure, we may have faults, but they aren't that bad. We see beams in other people's eyes and specks in our own, rather than the other way around. Someone else's quirks are glaring faults; ours are peccadilloes.

So, when judging our giving, we might be lenient with ourselves. We give enough, we'll say. It's too much trouble to actually look into the bottom line of what percent we give to the poor; we just have a feeling that it's plenty.

And maybe it is.

But maybe it isn't.

We are not going to know unless we examine ourselves thoroughly. Given the overall statistics, chances are pretty good that we're not doing as much as we can.

For example, the weekly parish contribution of Catholic families in the Archdiocese of Chicago is:

A. $20.

B. $10.

C. More than $20.

D. None of the above.

What do you think? How much does the average family give to its parish every week? Allow for the very rich and very poor to cancel each other out. How much does the majority (the affluent majority) give?

Or take the diocese of Rockville Centre, N.Y., a generally middle-class diocese of affluent people.

Do they give:
A. $50.
B. $25
C. $10
D. None of the above.

Or take a specific parish of 800 families in a suburb of an affluent city, a city which is always below the nationwide average in unemployment and which does not fall prey to the vagaries of lay-offs. How much does the average family give?
A. $20.
B. $15.
C. $10.
D. None of the above.

The answer, in each case, is D. And it is "none of the above" for the wrong reason: because it is far lower (not higher) than the other figures. In Chicago, the weekly figure is $2.44. In Rockville Centre, it is $2.02. In the affluent suburb, it is $2.25.

Admittedly that's taking all families and assuming they all give every week. But presume that half do not attend church or don't give. Double the figures and it is still a dismal commentary on support of the local parish community and its efforts in education, spiritual renewal, outreach to the poor, and maintenance of a religious presence in the neighborhood.

Catholics, accustomed to giving a buck a week for 20 years, have ignored the fact that inflation strikes at charities, too. The ludicrous sight of a family of five, making $25,000 annually and giving $2 a week to the parish, is all too common in America.

In another general statistic, the affluent do not turn out

too admirably either. According to IRS figures, people who earn the most contribute the smallest percentage of their income to charity. The gift may be larger, but, when it is compared with income, the percentage falls behind that of poorer people. For example, those whose annual gross income was from $4,000 to $6,000 donated approximately half as much to charity as those earning from $30,000 to $50,000. Their donations, though smaller, were proportionately much larger than those with the larger incomes.

Take your monthly income after deductions. Now add up your monthly expenses for essentials such as housing, utilities, food, and insurance. Subtract. What's left over? Your disposable income. What percent of it do you budget every month for the needy, for carrying out the work of justice? How much goes, every month, to your parish? To other charities? To groups working for the poor?

Is your individual answer more impressive than the general statistics?

7
What? Me Worry?

One of the most satisfying feelings in life is the one which comes when we do something we are obliged to do—and we end up being benefited ourselves.

For example, imagine that your parents asked you to clean out the attic, that catch-all which for years had been housing all the cast-offs of the family. Without much joy or anticipation, you go about the job—because you are obligated to.

But then, weeding through all the trash, you come across a treasure, some long-forgotten family heirloom. And it's yours for the finding. Because you did something for someone else, you were rewarded.

The same sort of thing can happen—on a much more sublime level—when we remember our obligation to the poor and to the work of justice. The reward is not a bentwood rocker or mantle clock; it is peace of mind.

One of the oldest truths of humanity (one contained in the myth of Midas) is that riches do not buy happiness. That simple fact is stated everywhere, in our most trivial songs ("The Best Things in Life are Free," "Can't Buy Me Love") and in our theaters ("J.B."), in the most banal of TV shows ("Dallas") and the most simple of fairy tales ("The Fisherman and His Wife"). That money cannot buy happiness has become a cliche, but that does not mean it is untrue; it means it has become generally accepted.

Furthermore, far from buying happiness, wealth cannot even stave off sadness. It sometimes seems, in fact, that money attracts woe. In an essay in *Time* magazine entitled "The Sad Truth About Big Spenders," the author writes, "It is not that the rich are any sadder than the rest of us, of course, but that they are so surprised at finding themselves sad at all. . . . Our hearts go out to these people because they suffer on our behalf. Most of us merely dream nonsense, but the rich have to live it; and while we rarely endure the consequences of our fantasies, they do so relentlessly."

Money, which solves so many petty problems of life (getting a seat in a crowded restaurant, finding a parking space, getting into the chic parties), is important in the face of the big problems. The entire Kennedy family is a testament to the failure of wealth to stave off misfortune. Their saga has been one of assassinations, retarded children, drug and alcohol abuse, alleged infidelity, manslaughter, and cancer. Like the barn-building tycoon in Jesus' parable, they have stored up all that the material world has to offer—and found it to be not enough. Peace of mind, contentment, equanimity, love, family closeness—these seem to elude the power of money. They are not displayed in a case in a jewelry store or offered in a catalog. And buying those things which are, it turns out, does not substitute for the possession of the "best things in life."

"Nothing that I worked for and earned meant a thing to me, because I knew that I would have to leave it to my successor and he might be wise or he might be foolish—who knows? . . . You work and worry your way through life, and what do you have to show for it? As long as you live, everything you do brings nothing but worry and heartache. Even at night your mind can't rest. . . . If you love money, you will never be satisfied; if you long to be rich, you will never get all you want. It is useless. The richer you are, the more mouths you have to feed. All you gain is the knowledge that you are rich. A working man may or may not have enough to eat, but at least he can get a good night's sleep. A rich man, however, has so much that he stays awake worrying. . . . Here is a terrible thing that I have seen in this world: people save up their money for a time when they need it, and then lose it all in some bad deal."

Who said that?

Some contemporary industrialist? A prince of some sheikdom? The king of England?

The lines are from the Bible: Ecclesiastes, a book which concerns itself with the uselessness of seeking fulfillment and perfection in things. Again and again, people have to discover that their wholeness will be found somewhere other than in what can be bought. In *Rerum Novarum,* Leo XIII reminds his readers of the "greed of possession and the thirst for pleasure—twin plagues, which too often make a man who is void of self-restraint miserable in the midst of abundance."

Miserable in the midst of abundance. Sad despite a big bank account. Plagued with physical ailments even though he has a Mercedes. Lonely and ignored even though she has a summer house on the Cape. How is it that such things happen? The poor often wonder about those with money. If I only had a little more, I would be content, says the poor man. But the affluent know better. We know that having a little more means having a little more to worry about. Jesus told us that it is difficult for the wealthy to get into heaven. Why? Because they have more to worry about, more to steward, more to dispense to the needy, more to decide how to use, more to consider the morality of.

Affluence brings worry with it, simply because we have so much more. Recall the lines of "I Got Plenty of Nothin'" from "Porgy and Bess": "I got no lock on the door; that's no way to be; they can steal the rug off the floor, 'cuz the things that I prize, like the stars in the skies, all are free."

But the affluent have locks on their doors and security systems and bank accounts and checking accounts and credit cards—and we worry about each one of them. Will someone steal my car? Is my Master Card still in my wallet? Where's the safest place to keep my valuables?

Affluence brings worry with it for another reason: we worry about whether we are living for our possessions or for the more important things of life. Affluence can tempt us to coat over our problems, to try to soothe our pains with "things." Chasing more money, the father who is never home to play with his son buys him a toy as a substitute. Never there to play catch, dad gives his boy a batting machine or an electronic football game. The wife who is caught up in her career buys her husband a new car stereo system. She gives him a sign of her love, instead of her love. The affluent couple in pursuit of more and more settles the problem of their elderly parents by sticking them in a nursing home. It costs a lot of money so it must be good—right?

Slowly the answer dawns on most of us. It is not right. Material things can never replace our personal presence and affection. We can't buy love, either for ourselves from others or for others in place of ourselves. And we worry.

Affluence brings worry with it for yet another reason:

We worry about how we are using the blessings we have been given. Are we living justly? The face of the starving child haunts us.

We worry.

We worry about our possessions. And if we have two cars, we have twice the worry.

We worry about others. How can we be with them when we're due to be at a meeting with a customer or the boss?

We worry about gaunt faces and swollen bellies.

We worry about the future, about keeping up our payments and keeping up our lifestyle, about the people from the cellar coming upstairs to take what is rightly theirs.

We worry and it nags at us, eats at us, stays with us. And we are not happy. We turn on the color TV and see an ad for CARE in which a bawling baby begs for milk from a mother nearly dead. We drive in our new car and it takes us past the ghetto with the crumbling homes and crumbling lives.

We worry and we are not happy. But then we make a discovery: by giving to others, by sharing, by being just, we become happy. Getting rid of some of our worries, we find a peace of mind, a spiritual calm, a sense of goodness which we never found in acquiring things.

Thus we find one more reason to give to others and perhaps the best reason of all—it makes us feel good. We have discovered the hidden treasure in the attic: amid all the junk, there is a gift; within the obligation lies a reward.

It turns out Shakespeare knew what he was talking about: "The quality of mercy is not strain'd

It droppeth as the gentle rain from heaven
Upon the place beneath: it is twice blest;
It blesseth him that gives and him that takes."

Justice blesses us as much as it blesses those we give to.

It also turns out that Jesus knew what he was talking about: "There is more happiness in giving than in receiving." (Acts 20:35)

There is something ennobling about being just. Like all virtues, justice is its own reward. We get when we give. We get freedom from worry and care, we get a sense of wholeness, we get a peek into heaven.

And by divesting ourselves of "things," we find out what is really important in life. Two young nurses who volunteered to leave their affluent homes and spend several months working in a Cambodian refugee camp came back happier than they had ever been before.

"We found out that we didn't need all the things we thought we needed," they reported. "We didn't need all the little electronic gimmicks and department store goods we had lived with all our lives. We were reduced to our most basic needs—food and shelter and other people—and we found that it was wonderful. You don't need all the things you think you need."

As Buddha put it, "If you have nothing, you have nothing to worry about."

But the affluent are tempted to collect all that they can, to build bigger barns and then buy better burglar alarm systems to protect the bigger barns. We buy a car and then worry someone will scratch it. We buy expensive china and then never use it for fear someone will break it. Affluence distracts us from thinking about what is essential in life. If we have to wash the car, we can't read the New Testament. If we have to meet with the insurance salesman, we can't play with our kids. If we have to stay late at the office, we can't be with our spouses.

Affluence makes us worry; affluence makes us unhappy; affluence takes us away from the center of our lives. By getting rid of affluence, we are being just and we will uncover a prize worth keeping.

By being just, by sharing our affluence, by protecting the natural resources, by conserving, by seeing to the spread of the intangible affluences, we will help ourselves by freeing us from worry, we will help our children by giving them a future and hope, and we will help everyone involved (us, our children, the poor) come closer to God.

8
Three Hard Questions

Three random questions for consideration by everyone who think about affluence, justice, and the poor:

1. How has modern medicine complicated the problem of justice?

People today live longer than ever before. That has created new problems for society and each individual: retirement, the needs of the elderly, nursing homes, medical costs into old age.

Living longer means needing more money. The affluent have to be concerned for the future as well as for today. When does preparing for retirement and old age sink into building bigger barns? To protect us into the golden years, we have to withhold more gold from the poor. The costs of living long—building retirement savings, paying for everything for more years, perhaps needing money for a nursing home or for private nursing, the cost of medical care as illnesses increase or lengthen in duration—are high.

The solution is not to die young. But there is a need to prudently prepare for old age while also seeing to the demands of justice.

How much can you keep aside for yourself? Can you depend on your children to support you? Should you depend on them or does that subtract from their own response to justice? Should you leave your money to your children or to the poor? Once you pass a certain age (say, you are 70 and your first-born is now 50), can you change your will to provide more for the needy and less for your children who are affluent themselves now?

2. To what extent can we depend on government and international agencies of government to do the work of justice?

This is a question, to some extent, of political leaning. It is the liberal view that government should be in the business of providing for the needy of the nation. This ranges from welfare programs to complete socialism. Through taxation, a great deal of the work of justice is carried out, but it is sometimes carried out bureaucratically and coldly. Those receiving the welfare are often treated as freeloaders and cheats; they are made to feel guilty about needing help.

A conservative view holds that it is more the business of private agencies (charities and religions) to provide for the needy. The government should stay out and concentrate more on providing a better economy, more jobs and material growth through private industry.

Can we let the government (the federal, state, county, or city government, or the United Nations) do the work of justice for us? Is it right to let it substitute for us? How much do we delegate to government? In what areas? Do we think of taxes as being justice-at-work or as being an act of highway robbery?

3. When can we say to ourselves, I gave enough?

The classic line to the doorstep solicitor—"I gave at the office"—represents the notion that there comes a point when we have given enough to the poor. Usually it doesn't mean we have given everything down to our essentials; it means we have given recently and don't want to give again.

Three Hard Questions

There are times when we are strapped and cannot respond to a charitable request. But is it always so when we refuse? Do we ever give enough?

I once watched as affluent women sorted through clothing donated to the poor. They were setting aside pieces of clothing for themselves and their relatives. Their rationale: "We've given enough to the poor; we figure it's time we got something in return."

9
Guilt and Giving

"I feel bad about the poor. It breaks my heart to see the films of the starving children. My husband and I try to do what we can. We give to the special collections at Mass and we give to whatever charities we can. But he doesn't make that much, and we have three children. Sometimes we barely make it from paycheck to paycheck.

"Then I think about the people who have no paychecks, and I feel guilty. We have so much, even though it's tough sometimes. And they have nothing at all. Are we doing enough?

"I know what Jesus said about helping the poor, and we do. But then I see another news story about the children in Africa, and I question myself. My husband and I talk about it. We feel guilty for having so much. What should we do?"

The preceding chapters in this book are in answer to this woman who once spoke to me about her feelings toward the poor. This chapter is an attempt to tell her, Don't feel guilty. If you are trying to help the poor, if you think of them, if you question yourself, then you are doing the work of justice. There is nothing to feel guilty about. In fact, there is a great deal to feel proud about.

It's easy, when confronted with the hard statistics of poverty, to feel guilty for having even the smallest something extra. And to be as affluent as most of America is leads to the temptation to feel great guilt. But we should not—unless we are wallowing in that luxury and ignoring the needy.

We do not have to reduce ourselves to sackcloth and sandals in order to help the poor. We don't have to cast ourselves into the gutter to feel better about helping them. All it takes to solve the woes of the poor is for everyone to do a little more.

"Sell all you have," Jesus told the rich young man. If that makes you feel guilty, look up the story of another wealthy man. (Luke 19) Zacchaeus was a short man who was long on money. He was a tax collector, a loathsome profession to the Jews who had to pay tribute to Rome. But he wanted to see Jesus and to know his teachings. So he climbed a tree to see above the heads of the taller people.

Spotting Zacchaeus, Jesus told him to come down and eat dinner with him. The followers of Jesus were scandalized. Was the teacher really going to eat with such a sinner?

Zacchaeus the short drew himself up to his full height. "I will give half of my belongings to the poor," he promised Jesus, "and I will repay those I have cheated four times what I took."

Jesus looked down at his new friend. "Salvation is yours," he said, "because the Son of Man came to save the lost."

The rich young man was told to give everything—because that's what it would have taken to be perfect. Zacchaeus gave half of his fortune—and that saved him. The poverty-stricken widow gave her only coins to the poor and that was enough while the rich man gave more coins but only a small percentage of his blessings—and that was not enough. (Mark 12:41 ff)

What must we give to be saved? That's for each person to determine alone and with his or her family. Jesus himself lived a simple, not a poverty-stricken, life. He had what he needed; he ate and drank; he slept beneath a roof and covered himself with a robe. He taught us to live the same way and to pray for "our daily bread."

Our daily bread is what we need to get by in life. What we need—not what we want. What we need varies with each person, but need is something each of us must examine. We cannot live haphazardly, taking what comes along without thought for others or without thought for what affluence does to us. Coming to a decision on what is enough is the work of prayer, study, thought, and discussion.

To help us, we have many examples of people who judged what their lives required. In the lives of the saints, we find case after case of people who chose simplicity over luxury and found in their choice their spiritual perfection.

Francis of Assisi, born rich, opened the New Testament one day and discovered that his life was headed in the wrong direction. Simplicity was what called him. So he rejected the affluent life and chose a life of simplicity.

Martin de Porres, born poor, worked among people like himself, bringing them comfort physically and spiritually.

Elizabeth Seton, born and wed wealthy, lost her fortune and chose to stay poor despite chances to regain affluence through marriage.

Thomas More, rich all his life, stayed that way and served God not only through charity but also through his intelligence and steadfastness.

There are all sorts of ways to God, all kinds of routes to take. When it comes to affluence, there are different methods of handling it justly. What matters is that we consider the options and choose; we cannot ignore the options and go along blissfully ignorant.

We should not feel guilty for being affluent. We should feel guilty for not using that affluence properly. Like all blessings, affluence itself is neutral. A person born with an ability to paint has a neutral blessing. He or she can use it properly—to inspire, amuse, and enlighten others—or improperly—to propagandize, to titillate, and to ridicule. It is the use that matters.

Born with great beauty, a woman can become a leader or a temptress. Born with a powerful voice, a man can become a speaker of truth or a demagogue. Born into affluence, we can become people of justice or misers. The guilt comes from the wrong choice. Making the right choice (to be people of justice) should never lead us to feel guilty or unworthy or weak.

On the contrary, being just should make us feel proud. We should let others know in hopes of showing them what they can do. I recall a cartoon in *The New Yorker.* It showed a husband and wife in the kitchen getting drinks for their guests. The rooms were obviously those of an upwardly mobile couple, stylish and chic. The wife whispered to her husband, "Now, for God's sake, don't start telling everyone how little we paid for everything."

Actually, we *should* tell people how little we paid for everything and how much we gave to the needy. We should do this not to blow our own horns or to make them feel bad, but to invite them to join us and to know how good they can feel when they share.

The elemental lesson of childhood—to share with others—should carry over into our adult lives. The sandbox at the playground or the world itself: in both places, we should move over and make room, we should pass around the toys we have, we should help our neighbors fill their pails.

The contentment and peace and fulfillment we seek in life can be found when we call down the steps and invite the folks in the cellar to come join us upstairs.

10
Small Steps and Giant Leaps

There is a challenging phrase in the documents of the Second Vatican Council. We have already quoted it, but this time we can pay special attention to one point. In "The Church Today," the Council spoke about the right of the poor to a share in the world's goods.

"The Fathers and Doctors of the Church," the document proceeds, "held this view, teaching that men are obliged to come to the relief of the poor, and *to do so not merely out of their superfluous goods.*"

Not out of our surplus and left-overs. Not out of our extras. Not out of what is left after we have subtracted what we need. But out of our substance, out of our needs, out of what we require.

During his visit to the United States, Pope John Paul II, addressing crowds in Yankee Stadium, said this:

"We cannot stand idly by when thousands of human beings are dying of hunger. Nor can we remain indifferent when the rights of the human spirit are trampled upon. . . . We cannot stand idly by, enjoying our own riches and freedom, if, in any place, the Lazarus of the 20th century stands at our doors. (That parable) must always be present in our memory, it must form our conscience. Christ demands openness to our brothers and sisters in need—openness from the rich, the affluent, the economically advanced, openness to the poor, the underdeveloped, and the disadvantaged.

"The poor are our brothers and sisters. You must never be content to leave them just the crumbs from the feast. *You must take of your substance, and not just of your abundance,* in order to help them."

This is a stronger demand than previous remarks of the church on our duty toward the poor; it is a challenging call to us. It means donating our new coat, not the old one in the closet; giving a new pair of shoes, not the ones we would throw out otherwise; handing over to the poor part of our savings, not just part of our disposable income. It is a radical call to do more than ever before.

The seriousness of the current world situation is the reason for the call:

- Six percent of the world's population consumes 40 percent of the world's goods
- 1.7 million people died of starvation, malnutrition, and lack of water in Africa in one year alone
- 30 children die every minute of malnutrition
- More than 12 million children died in one year of hunger-related diseases

To set the balance right—to bring justice into the world—we must make a stand now. That stand means deciding in favor of justice and the poor. It means changing ourselves a little bit for them.

The call to give of our substance cannot be heeded until we give of our affluence. We must take small steps first; the giant strides will come in time. We are not called to turn our lives around in one afternoon; God leads us slowly and by inches until one day we turn around to look at where we used to be and find that it is far in the distance and long ago in time.

The Council's and the Pope's desire that we give from our substance emphasizes how serious the demands of justice are. To answer those demands, we have to begin now. We have to begin to think, to analyze our own situation, to apply some of the suggestions in this book, to discuss the topic with others, to meditate on it ourselves, to pray. This will lead us to a decision, to a first step.

There is nothing magic about doing God's work on earth. We will not wake up one morning and decide to become the next St. Francis. But, if we want to and if we work at it, we will wake up morning after morning with the knowledge that we are carrying out Jesus' teaching on our duty toward the poor. Those mornings will add up to a person who is holier and whole-er, to a feeling of accomplishment and peace, to a sense of having done what is right.

The longest journey, the proverb says, begins with the first step. It is that step we must take in hopes that one will lead to another and another until we see Jesus in the poor and his grace in our work.

I was hungry and you fed me;
I was thirsty and you gave me drink;
I was a stranger and you received me in your homes;
I was naked and you clothed me;
I was sick and you took care of me;
I was in prison and you visited me.

Whenever you did this for one of the least important of these brothers of mine, you did it for me. (Matthew 25: 35-40)

When we do the work of justice, we do it for the poor, for ourselves, and for Jesus. We bless the poor, free ourselves, and follow Jesus.

In the house of the world, it is time to open the cellar door and let Jesus come up.